A Literary Tour *of*
GLOUCESTERSHIRE AND BRISTOL

A Literary Tour *of*

GLOUCESTERSHIRE AND BRISTOL

David Carroll

ALAN SUTTON

First published in the United Kingdom in 1994
Alan Sutton Publishing Ltd
Phoenix Mill · Far Thrupp · Stroud · Gloucestershire

First published in the United States of America in 1994
Alan Sutton Publishing Inc
83 Washington Street · Dover · NH 03820

British Library Cataloguing in Publication Data

A catalogue record for this book is available from the British
Library

ISBN 0-7509-0228-0

Library of Congress Cataloging in Publication Data applied for

Cover illustration: Elegant Women in a Library, *Edouard
Gelhay (b. 1856) (Waterhouse and Dodd, London;
photograph: Bridgeman Art Library)*

Typeset in 11/14 Sabon.
Typesetting and origination by
Alan Sutton Publishing Limited.
Printed in Great Britain by
Redwood Books, Trowbridge.

For Henry Malcolm Carroll (1920–1992)

Contents

Contents

Illustrations

Illustrations

Foreword

It may prove helpful to explain this book's arrangement. In the first place it consists of a more-or-less circular and clockwise literary tour of Gloucestershire as a whole, starting and finishing at one of the county's most famous natural landmarks, May Hill. Partly because they did not fit in neatly with this scheme of things, but mainly because each demanded detailed attention in its own right, Cheltenham, Gloucester and Bristol have all been accorded separate chapters, following the end of the tour.

Gloucestershire and Bristol are fortunate in being particularly well-endowed with literary connections; to such a degree, in fact, that there can be few counties or cities in England so well placed in this respect. Over the years they have nourished not only a great outpouring of native talent – Thomas Chatterton, Robert Southey, Ivor Gurney, Laurie Lee and all the rest – but also drawn like a magnet countless distinguished literary visitors. Some, such as Daniel Defoe, Charles Dickens and Beatrix Potter, were transient, while many others, including Samuel Taylor Coleridge, John Masefield, W.H. Davies and Evelyn Waugh, lingered long, in some cases for many years. Altogether the list of such visitors reads, as Lady Cynthia Asquith would put it, like scores of items out of *Who's Who*.

No survey of any county's literary connections could claim to be definitive where, as in the present case, conscious omissions have been made for reasons of balance, proportion and space, and where unconscious omissions (although hopefully few) have been perpetrated through ignorance. Furthermore, a different writer tackling the same theme might well have chosen to emphasize matters that I have skated over, and vice versa. Nevertheless, I trust that the following account represents a full and accurate picture of the literary landscape of Gloucestershire and Bristol.

I am grateful to many people for their help during the preparation of this book, particularly to those individuals who, occupying houses with a literary significance, were kind enough to provide me with photographs of their homes. I owe a special debt to Leslie Knight of Dumbleton, David Evans of Dursley, Mrs Betty Merrett of Stroud and Mrs S.L. Fletcher of Charlton Kings for their various contributions to the photographic content of this book.

Above all I am grateful to Bernadette Walsh for a judicious mixture of advice and encouragement dispensed when it was most needed.

Acknowledgements

I should like to thank the following for granting permission to quote from copyright material:

In and Out of the Forest (1984), Winifred Foley and Century Hutchinson; *Grace Before Ploughing* (1967), 'The Everlasting Mercy' and 'Daffodil Fields', the Society of Authors, on behalf of the estate of John Masefield; *A Cotswold Year* (1936), the estate of C. Henry Warren; *The Selected Letters of Robert Frost* (1965), L. Thompson (Ed.) and Jonathan Cape; 'The Empty Cottage' and 'The Golden Room', the estate of Wilfred Gibson and Macmillan; *Edward Thomas: the Last Four Years* (1958), the estate of Eleanor Farjeon and Oxford University Press; 'The Thatch', the estate of Robert Frost; *Portrait of Elmbury* (1945) and *Brensham Village* (1946), the estate of John Moore; *A Life of Contrasts* (1977), Diana Mosley and Hamish Hamilton; *The Letters of Mrs Gaskell* (1966), J.A.V. Chapple & A. Pollard (Eds) and Manchester University Press; 'Dumbleton Hall' and 'Summoned by Bells', the estate of Sir John Betjeman and John Murray; *Portrait of Barrie* (1954), the estate of Cynthia Asquith and James Barrie; 'Burnt Norton', the estate of T.S. Eliot and Faber & Faber; *English Journey* (1934) and *Good Companions* (1929), the estate of J.B. Priestley and William Heinemann; 'Chipping Campden', the Society of Authors, on behalf of the estate of John Masefield; *By Chance I Did Rove* (1951), the estate of Nancy Jewson; *Men and Memories* (1978), the estate of William Rothenstein and Chatto & Windus; 'Same Cottage, but another Song of

Acknowledgements

another Season', Mrs Eva Reichmann, on behalf of the Max Beerbohm estate; *The Journal of Beatrix Potter* (1966), Leslie Linder (transcriber) and Frederick Warne; *Cider With Rosie* (1959), Laurie Lee and The Hogarth Press; *As I Walked Out One Midsummer Morning* (1969), Laurie Lee and Penguin; Brian Waters's introduction to *The Essential W.H. Davies* (1951), Jonathan Cape; *The Diaries of Evelyn Waugh* (1976), M. Davies (Ed.), the estate of Evelyn Waugh and Weidenfeld & Nicolson; *The Letters of Evelyn Waugh* (1980), M. Amory (Ed.), the estate of Evelyn Waugh and Weidenfeld & Nicolson; *Portrait of a Country Neighbour* (1967), Frances Donaldson and Weidenfeld & Nicolson; *The White Sparrow* (1954), the estate of John Moore; *A Child in the Forest* (1974), Winifred Foley and Oxford University Press; 'Solitary Confinement', 'My Village' and 'Rondel of Gloucestershire', the estate of F.W. Harvey and Sidgwick & Jackson; 'Do you Remember Adlestrop', from *Sea to the West* (1981), the estate of Norman Nicolson and Faber & Faber; *A Fool in the Forest* and 'Early Portrait', the literary executor of Leonard Clark; *The Ordeal of Ivor Gurney* (1978), Michael Hurd and Oxford University Press.

Picture Credits

The sources of the illustrations used in this book are as follows:

p. 6 Mrs Simon Skelding; pp. 22, 27 & 47 Gloucestershire Record Office; p. 31 Leslie Knight; pp. 37 & 59 Corinium Museum, Cirencester; p. 52 Stow-on-the-Wold & District Civic Society; pp. 64 & 67 Illustrations Collection, Cirencester Bingham Library; pp. 74 & 86 Mrs B. Merrett; p. 79 Robert Hutton; p. 85 Mrs R. Marwood; p. 89 Charles Stuart-Menteth; p. 93 Mrs Joan Sanderson; p. 107 David Evans; pp. 124 & 136 Cheltenham Art Gallery and Museums; pp. 128 & 134 lent by the late John Williams; p. 131 The headmaster, Dean Close School; p. 139 Mr & Mrs J.S. Harrison; pp. 144 & 147 Gloucestershire Collection, Gloucester City Library; pp. 161, 163, 168, 183 & 187 Bristol Museums and Art Gallery; pp. 177 & 189 Bristol Record Office. All remaining photographs were taken by the author.

A LITERARY MAP OF GLOUCESTERSHIRE AND BRISTOL
(Not to scale)

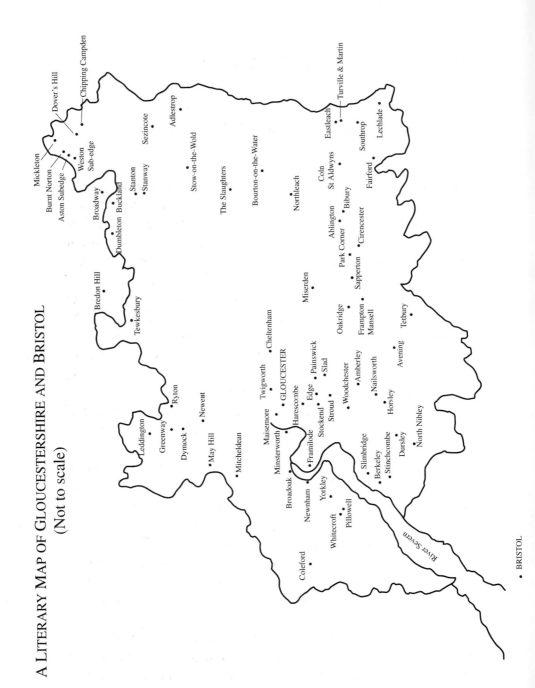

CHAPTER ONE

From May Hill . . .

For hillwalkers in remote, boulder-strewn landscapes, cairns are usually a welcome sight, appearing as signposts along the route to the summit or as beacons on the way back home. The Lakeland fells or the Black Mountains may seem a far remove from the more gentle, undulating contours of Gloucestershire, but here, too, a point appears against the horizon to provide just as effective a guiding star as any of those small pyramids of stones. For there could hardly be a more fitting place in the whole of the county to begin a literary journey than May Hill, that 'half-revealed, tree-clad thing', as the native Gloucestershire poet, Ivor Gurney, called it, which is arguably the county's most distinctive and potent landmark. It stands just under a thousand feet high and about three miles north-east of Mitcheldean, its north-western flank tumbling down to the border with Hereford and Worcester.

May Hill's famous crown of huge pine trees, which stand in close ranks on the deceptively exposed summit, can be seen far and wide. Winifred Foley compares them to the gaze of the Mona Lisa so that, 'wherever you are within a radius of many miles, those trees seem to be keeping an eye on you'. They are a symbol of home for anyone brought up within sight of them, which must include many thousands of people, for it is said that on a clear day you can see twelve counties from the top of May Hill.

For one embryo poet, at least, living in 'Paradise', as he always described it, at Ledbury, in the closing decades of the nineteenth century, May Hill made a deep and lasting

The summit of May Hill, that 'half-revealed, tree-clad thing'

impression throughout a long life. John Masefield, who spent his early years playing on the banks of the Hereford–Gloucester canal, where its barges, 'carrying hearts of gold and cargoes of wonder', were a source of endless fascination to him, wrote in extreme old age about the impression May Hill had made on him as a child in the 1880s:

> The hill, I suppose, would be about seven miles from us, and, at that distance, it gave to us, on any clear day, a most vivid image of a man ploughing with a yoked team. No one could be in any doubt that at the top of the hill, facing the distant River Severn, (due south), a giant ploughman drove a team that never got any further. The grown-up observer knew that the ploughman, the plough and the team were distant trees, but the little child thought that they were real ploughing figures, and giant figures . . .

Recalling a child's enthusiasm for the macabre, he went on to describe how it was still possible when he was a lad to 'grub up' small cannonballs that had been embedded on the slopes of May Hill since the days when a battle in the Civil War had been fought there. More darkly still, he told how it was also possible to find bits of old highwaymen, who had been hanged on the gibbet that once stood on the hillside!

These recollections of Masefield's childhood spent on the Herefordshire/Gloucestershire border, can be found in his fragment of autobiography, *Grace Before Ploughing*, which appeared in 1967, the year of his death. It was more than half a century earlier, however, that the poet had first likened May Hill's 'topknot' to a ploughman, in his narrative poem, 'The Everlasting Mercy'. Written and published in 1911, it tells the story of Saul Kane, a Ledbury rogue and drunkard who experiences a religious conversion and settles down to the life of an honest ploughman. The erstwhile roaring boy shared the same natural landmarks that dominated Masefield's earliest years:

> I've marked the May Hill ploughman
> There on his hill, day after day
> Driving his team against the sky . . .

In 1933, shortly after he had chosen to make his home in Gloucestershire, for a while at least, Masefield, who was by now a celebrated literary figure and the Poet Laureate, became involved in a scheme to buy Pauntley Court, a couple of miles to the north of Newent and lying close to May Hill. The manor house, built around a small courtyard and nestling in a shallow well of land on a hilltop, with a medieval, four-gabled dovecote and old Pauntley church for company, stands in the heart of the still beautiful but now sadly diminished daffodil fields that were once such a feature of that north-western corner of Gloucestershire. In a memorable poem, simply called 'Daffodil

Fields', Masefield describes a once familiar scene in the area at daffodil-picking time:

> And there the pickers come, picking for town
> Those dancing daffodils; all day they pick;
> Hard-featured women, weather-beaten brown,
> Or swarthy-red, the colour of old brick.

C. Henry Warren, writing in *A Cotswold Year*, recalled a spring afternoon at nearby Dymock during the 1930s when he came

> upon the crowds, crowds out in the fields picking; crowds in the roadway loading up their treasure. In all the people numbered several hundreds, and yet the fields still looked as full of flowers as if nobody had come this way at all. It was a carnival of Spring.

The proposal to create a Home for Wayfarers at Pauntley Court to accommodate some of Gloucestershire's unemployed and homeless youngsters was something that quickly caught Masefield's attention. At the age of eighteen or nineteen he had found himself in a similar position in New York, having jumped ship after deciding that he did not want to follow a seafaring career. He worked briefly in a bar before finding a full-time job in a carpet factory at Yonkers, where he lodged with the family of a fellow employee.

Masefield never forgot how lucky he had been to find his feet again, and often thought how differently his life might have turned out. In the prospectus for the scheme he wrote:

> Like many lads in England today, I set out penniless from my last shelter and tramped along the road looking for work . . . I know to this day how lucky I felt that I found work, and what kind of life I should have had, if the luck had been witheld.

As a part of his contribution towards raising the £2,000 needed for the purchase of Pauntley Court, Masefield gave countless readings of his own poetry throughout Gloucestershire. He also drafted letters of appeal to likely subscribers, in which he outlined the plight of the many young boys who spent their days tramping along the county's roads looking for employment, and who slept at night in the local workhouse. 'If you will establish a Home where they may find shelter, work and encouragement to a fresh start,' he wrote earnestly, 'you will save a fellow-countryman from the despair and degredation which are not so much their fault as our disgrace.' At a fund-raising meeting in Bristol in 1933 he described Pauntley as a spot

> where I have spent some of the happiest years of my life . . . it has been a place of deep delight to me in childhood and later. It lies in a place of great beauty and strangeness, very dear to me.

Having been brought up just a few miles away at Ledbury, it seems that Masefield must have known the Butler family, who were at Pauntley Court throughout his childhood.

In February 1934 the Poet Laureate finally achieved his personal target of raising £750 towards the project with a reading given at the Royal Agricultural College, Cirencester. Meanwhile the first five young 'wayfarers' had been received at Pauntley Court during the previous September but, unfortunately, the home was closed down in 1940 and requisitioned for wartime use. The recreation room (which the present owners call the ballroom) is dedicated to Masefield's memory in recognition of the generous help he gave to buy the property.

* * *

It did not pass unnoticed by Masefield that Pauntley Court was associated with the birth of Dick Whittington, whose ghost the

Pauntley Court, Newent, c. 1930

Poet Laureate did not scruple to invoke in his letter of appeal
for the purchase of the manor house. 'I like to think,' he told
potential donors, 'that the lads who enter the home will go
from it re-made and not do less well than Whittington.'

The passage of time has been even more effective than usual
in drawing a veil over the details of Whittington's life.
However, his pantomime persona is probably the most familiar
one: that of the poor boy who went to London to make his
fortune and who, after despairing of ever doing so, rose to
become the most famous of lord mayors – with the assistance
of his cat! But that, of course, is the Dick Whittington of
pantomime.

The real-life Richard Whittington was born in the late
1350s. His father, Sir William Whittington, was a London
mercer who owned old Pauntley Court, the predecessor of the
present eighteenth-century house where, incidentally, some
remains of the original, fourteenth-century building can still be
seen. Just how much of his childhood the lad spent in
Gloucestershire is open to conjecture. All that we can be
certain of is that, because his father was not particularly

wealthy and he was the youngest son, Richard was apprenticed (after Sir William's death) to a London merchant, and soon became an immensely successful businessman in his own right: 'the model merchant of the Middle Ages', as the eighteenth-century archaeologist Samuel Lysons described him. He served three terms as Lord Mayor of London and was a liberal benefactor to the city providing, among other things, a much needed piped water supply, and leaving a legacy for the rebuilding of Newgate Prison.

Whittington died in 1423, but the popular legend of Whittington and his cat was not licensed for the press until almost two hundred years later, in 1605, thereby allowing plenty of time for any number of apocryphal stories to gather around him. The greatest mystery, and yet an essential ingredient of the pantomime, of course, is the role of Whittington's cat. The idea of a cat making its owner's fortune is certainly not unique, as it occurs in a number of ancient European folk-tales, but this aspect of the story does at least require some explanation.

The fanciful notion that Whittington lent his cat to a Moorish prince who wanted to rid his palace of rats, and was then handsomely rewarded when the job had been done successfully, is clearly just a part of the Whittington legend. A more plausible explanation, it has been suggested, might be that the cat was not really a cat at all but originally, perhaps, a ship with a name that sounded something like 'cat'; one of the vessels, in fact, on which the immense fortune of Richard Whittington, native of Gloucestershire and merchant of London, was founded.

CHAPTER TWO

A Poets' Holiday

The mainly brick and half-timber village of Dymock lies about three miles west of Pauntley Court along the banks of the River Leadon. John Kyrle, the so-called 'Man of Ross', was born here at The White House in 1637, but he spent most of his prodigiously long life in Ross-on-Wye. Here his numerable charitable enterprises eventually came to the notice of the eighteenth-century poet Alexander Pope, who mentioned him in his Epistle, 'Of the Use of Riches', dedicated to the first Earl Bathurst of Cirencester Park:

> Rise, honest Muse! and sing the Man of Ross,
> The Man of Ross divides the weekly bread:
> He feeds yon Alms-house, neat, but void of state,
> Where Age and Want sit smiling at the gate . . .
> Is any sick? the Man of Ross relieves,
> Prescribes, attends, the med'cine makes, and gives.

Visitors to Dymock's Norman parish church, however, will discover a more recent literary connection with the village. A corner at the west end of St Mary's is devoted to a permanent exhibition celebrating the life and work of a small group of poets who came to settle and write in the Leadon Valley just before the First World War. None of them actually lived in Dymock itself, but they were scattered around the parish in various hamlets: at Ryton, Leddington and Greenway Cross.

Lascelles Abercrombie had been the first to arrive, in 1911, drawn to Ryton from his native Ashton-on-Mersey by a love for the area that had developed when he was a schoolboy at Malvern College. Born in 1881, he started work as a trainee quantity surveyor in Liverpool but quickly turned to literary journalism. He began writing poetry, and his first book, *Interlude and Poems*, appeared in 1908. When his sister married a farmer and settled at Much Marcle (just over the Herefordshire border) in 1910, it gave Abercrombie an opportunity to search for a home of his own in the locality, and he moved into The Gallows the following year. Recalling those days in a later autobiographical essay, he enthused:

> Here I am in a cottage in Gloucestershire, living the life (or very nearly) I have always wanted to live! – How did that happen? I scarcely know . . . the opening came, and without stopping to think, I broke away and ran.

The Gallows, in fact, was a pair of cottages converted into one, with a thatched roof and a garden which, according to John Haines, the Gloucester solicitor, botanist and poet, was the most beautiful he had ever seen.

Next came the Northumberland poet Wilfred Gibson who was easily tempted away from the London garret where he was then living – a shabby room above Harold Monro's poetry bookshop in Bloomsbury's Devonshire Street – by Abercrombie's boundless enthusiasm for his Gloucestershire idyll. Gibson, who was born at Hexham in 1878, stayed for a while with his friend at The Gallows during the summer of 1913, before settling a few months later into The Old Nail Shop, a partly thatched, timber-and-brick cottage two miles away at Greenway Cross.

It was Gibson, in fact, who persuaded the American poet Robert Frost to swap the suburban bungalow he was renting at that time just outside London for the delights of the genuine countryside. Frost, who was slightly older than Gibson and Abercrombie, came to England with his family in 1912, mainly

The Old Nail Shop, Greenway Cross

because publishers for his work were proving elusive in the United States. It was a wise move: his first two volumes of poems, *A Boy's Will* (1913) and *North of Boston* (1914), were published in England, the latter, which contains 'The Death of the Hired Man', securing for him an international reputation. A cottage called Little Iddens was found for the Frosts at Leddington, to the north of Greenway Cross, and they moved into it during the early summer of 1914. That May Frost wrote enthusiastically to a friend:

> This is a great change from Beaconsfield which was merely suburban. We are now in the country, the cider country, where we have to keep a barrel of cider for our visitors and our hired help, or we will have no visitors nor hired help . . .

With Frost's migration to Gloucestershire, the hard core of the 'Dymock Poets' was established, although the colony was by no means complete. Edward Thomas, Rupert Brooke and John

Drinkwater were three visitors who were to become closely associated with the group, a connection that in Thomas's case, through his friendship with Frost, did much to help him discover his true vocation as a poet. For a few years this quiet corner, hitherto known chiefly for its fine cider, was firmly on the literary map as often during the summer months various friends and acquaintances – including fellow poets Ivor Gurney, W.H. Davies and John Masefield, and the children's authors Arthur Ransome and Eleanor Farjeon – arrived to take long country walks by day, and to argue endlessly about poetry in lamp-lit cottages at night.

The majority of those poets who were closely associated with what the Reverend Gethyn-Jones, a local vicar, later described as 'The Muse Colony' were significantly affected by the months and, in some cases, the years they spent at Dymock. For Abercrombie and Gibson, in particular, this 'poets' holiday' (as Thomas's wife, Helen, called it) in the Leadon Valley produced their most lasting work, much of which was inspired by their immediate surroundings. Abercrombie wrote prolifically while living at The Gallows, and in 'Ryton Firs', he produced a fine poem with a subject on his own doorstep: a wood at the back of his cottage. The first stanza begins with these memorable lines:

> Dear boys, they've killed our woods, the ground
> Now looks ashamed, to be shorn so bare.
> Naked lank ridge and brooding mound
> Seem shivering cowed in the April air.

Later, he too mentions the daffodil fields, obviously relishing the litany of place-names in the process:

> . . . From Marcle way,
> From Dymock, Kempley, Newent, Bromsberrow,
> Redmarley, all the meadowland daffodils seem
> Running in golden tides to Ryton Firs . . .

Gibson's themes – although much of his work before and after the Dymock interlude was heavily influenced by his northern background – were sometimes even closer to home. He wrote three poems about The Old Nail Shop itself, the saddest of which is undoubtedly 'The Empty Cottage', silent and deserted when the rhythm of life at Dymock is interrupted by war:

> Lonely and empty it stands
> By the signpost that stretches white hands,
> Pointing to far-away lands
> Where alone and apart we are lying.

However, while Gibson and Abercrombie are hardly remembered today and their work is much neglected, Frost went on to become one of the most popular of twentieth-century American poets. He spent a year in Gloucestershire before returning to the United States in February 1915. For part of the time he too lived at Ryton, his own family – his wife, Elinor, and four children – sharing The Gallows with the Abercrombies and their young sons. Both there and at Little Iddens the hallmark of the Frosts' existence was informality, as Farjeon described in her account of Thomas's last years:

The Frosts did not live by the clock, their clock conformed to the Frosts . . . Meals (bedtimes, too, I believe) were when you felt like them . . . When the children were hungry enough to be more interested in eating than in what they were doing, they came indoors and helped themselves . . . The centre of the Frosts was out-of-doors . . .

The impact of those twelve months at Dymock on Frost's poetry is always difficult to measure. His poem 'After Apple Picking' might well reflect living in a cider-making district, and 'The Thatch', written in 1928, may have some connection with

Little Iddens, Leddington

the later ruinous condition of The Gallows, a cottage of which he was particularly fond (although it was reported that when Frost visited Dymock for the last time, in 1957, the elderly poet had been visibly moved on his arrival at Little Iddens and The Old Nail Shop, but seemed relatively untouched by his return to the site of the Abercrombies' former home at Ryton):

> They tell me the cottage where we dwelt,
> Its wind-torn thatch now goes unmended;
> Its life of hundreds of years has ended . . .

But Frost was more of a true countryman than either Gibson or Abercrombie, and his old home in rural New England exerted a powerful influence over him. He wrote a great deal while living in Gloucestershire, no doubt inspired by surroundings so congenial to his nature. But, as Keith Clark points out in his book *The Muse Colony* (1992), in Frost's poem 'The Sound of the Trees', for example, the American apparently had in mind not only some trees near The Gallows but also others in New England.

There is no doubt at all, however, that Frost played an important part during the summer of 1914 in shaping Thomas's future career as a poet. The two men had already met and become close friends in London, so that when Frost moved to Gloucestershire Thomas was soon drawn to visit him there. After staying at The Gallows on several occasions during the spring, Thomas spent the whole of August, with his wife and family, at Oldfields, a farmhouse just a few meadows away from Little Iddens. Writing in *The Times* at the beginning of August 1963, Helen Thomas recalled that holiday taken half a century earlier, and the nature of her husband's friendship with the New England poet:

> They were always together, and when not exploring the country they sat in the shade of a tree talking endlessly of literature and of poetry in particular . . . Robert encouraged Edward – who had not written any poetry – to think of himself as a potential poet.

A few months after the holiday had come to an end, Thomas captured the flavour of those days with Frost in verse:

> The sun used to shine while we two walked
> Slowly together, paused and started
> Again, and sometimes mused, sometimes talked
> As either pleased, and cheerfully parted
> Each night . . .

Born in 1878, Thomas was prone to bouts of deep depression and was always battling to make ends meet financially. He was a highly respected critic, but the writing of mainly topographical and biographical prose, which had occupied him for most of his literary career, left him drained and desperately unfulfilled. It comes as something of a disappointment, therefore, when leafing through Thomas's delightful book *A Literary Pilgrim in England,* for example, to realize that he derived little, if any, pleasure from writing it. It was Frost who, during those long walks in the woods, meadows and orchards around Leddington, did so much to release the latent poet in Thomas. In 1921 Frost wrote:

> I bantered, teased and bullied all the summer we were together at Leddington and Ryton. It was plain that he had wanted to be a poet all the years he had been writing about poets not worth his little finger.

Frost's encouragement and advice, given as it was during those dying days of peace in the late summer of 1914, did not come a moment too soon. Shortly afterwards Thomas did indeed seriously begin writing poetry, and contributed his work to various periodicals under the pseudonym 'Edward Eastaway'. In 1916 a privately printed volume, *Six Poems,* appeared, and it was followed by a larger collection in 1917. By that time, however, Thomas had already been killed in the Battle of Arras. It is sad to reflect that most of his poetry, the work that gave him the greatest satisfaction and for which he is best remembered, was published posthumously.

Farjeon, who spent a brief holiday at Leddington in late August 1914 as a result of her friendship with the Thomases, has left an amusing account of one aspect of the poets' social life at Dymock. She lodged at a farmhouse called Glyn Iddens, just a short step along the lane from Little Iddens, where she was looked after by a Mr and Mrs Farmer, and was provided with an endless stream of home-made cider. Mrs Farmer, according to Farjeon, 'had stepped out of a chapter by George Eliot, her husband out of another by Thomas Hardy, and they

Glyn Iddens, Leddington

had joined forces midway; it was obvious who was captain of the ship'.

As such, Mrs Farmer enlisted Farjeon's help in inviting all the 'Dymock Poets' to a meal at Glyn Iddens one evening. After a gargantuan farmhouse dinner, which was rounded off with a huge Stilton and washed down, inevitably, with cider, it was time to go home. Farjeon recalled:

> The poets attempted to rise, but the gallons of strong cider, against which I had been inoculated, had gone to their legs, and not one of them could stand without support. I saw Edward and Robert stagger to their feet, clutch each other and go down; they rose again with great caution, clinging together. On the other side of the table, Gibson and Abercrombie were behaving similarly. Two brace of poets staggered out into the moonlight and went hilariously

homeward like two sets of Siamese twins. I have boasted ever since of the night when I drank all the poets in Gloucestershire under the table.

However, in between long walks and endless discussions about poetry, not to mention apple-picking and cider-drinking, the 'Dymock Poets' actually got down to some very serious work, not least the publication of four issues of *New Numbers*, a quarterly magazine, which was printed in Gloucester and despatched to subscribers at home and overseas from the tiny post office at Dymock. It comprised work not only by Abercrombie and Gibson, but also by Brooke and Drinkwater, who, as friends of Abercrombie's, had both visited The Gallows at various times. The final issue, which appeared early in 1915, contained Brooke's five 'War Sonnets', including 'The Soldier' ('If I should die, think only this of me . . .'). *New Numbers*, although short-lived, was highly regarded and each issue was eagerly anticipated by the more discerning poetry-reading public.

It was the outbreak of the First World War that caused the various poets who had gathered around Dymock to disperse. Within a few years both Brooke and Thomas were dead – Brooke died of blood-poisoning on his way to the Dardanelles in April 1915 and Thomas was killed in action two years later – but their reputations as poets were to flourish. Abercrombie and Gibson, however, never again enjoyed the degree of literary success they had achieved while living in Gloucestershire. Abercrombie went on to build a distinguished academic career, which included posts as Professor of Poetry at Leeds University and Reader in English at Oxford, before his death in 1938. He wrote a number of critical studies, but almost entirely abandoned poetry. Gibson, however, continued to publish verse; one critic rather unkindly remarked that his work would have been more effective had there been less of it! His final volume, *Within Four Walls*, appeared in 1950.

Meanwhile Drinkwater established a successful career for himself in the theatre and Frost became a 'grand old man' of American letters.

Later, both Gibson and Abercrombie looked back nostalgically over the years to those halcyon days before the storm broke over Europe. In 'The Golden Room' Gibson fondly recalled just one of many evenings when the poets congregated at The Old Nail Shop:

> . . . In the lamplight
> We talked and laughed, but, for the most part, listened
> While Robert Frost kept on and on and on,
> In his slow New England fashion, for our delight . . .

Abercrombie reflected on the enormous pleasure it had given him to have Gibson and Frost for his neighbours, and to share a jug of cider in his garden with Brooke and Thomas. 'I make no cider now,' he wrote wistfully, in 1932, 'and I have no garden. But once I lived in Gloucestershire.'

CHAPTER THREE

Tewkesbury

Were Lascelles Abercrombie still living at Ryton today those balmy summer evenings spent in the garden of The Gallows with his friends might well be accompanied by the occasional low moan of traffic from the nearby M50. A few miles' drive eastwards along the motorway would bring him to Tewkesbury, a town that was bypassed when the railways came, but which now rests in the crook of the elbow formed by the M5 and its spur to Ross-on-Wye.

Tewkesbury has laboured under more than one literary pseudonym in its time. For readers of nineteenth-century fiction and of one novel in particular, Mrs Craik's *John Halifax, Gentleman*, this delightful old north-Gloucestershire town, by the confluence of the Severn and the Avon, will always be Norton Bury. To aficionados of John Moore's 'Brensham' trilogy, however – written and published during the 1940s – it could never be anything other than Elmbury.

The dominating presence in Tewkesbury, of course, looming high above the many Tudor rooftops of the town, is the abbey church of St Mary the Virgin with its square Norman tower, the largest of its kind still in existence; and a seventeenth-century organ, originally owned by Oliver Cromwell, which had been played by the poet John Milton when the instrument was housed at Hampton Court Palace. Not surprisingly, perhaps, the abbey arrested the attention of many early visitors, among them Daniel Defoe, the author of *Robinson Crusoe*, who rode through Tewkesbury on his way from Gloucester to Worcester during his *Tour through the Whole*

Island of Great Britain. Although these accounts of his travels – comprising an early and important national survey, written with the eye of a keen journalist – were published in three volumes between 1724 and 1726 (and only a few years prior to Defoe's death in 1731), the visit would certainly have taken place some years earlier. Defoe paused only long enough to record a few brief impressions of this 'large and very populous town situate upon the River Avon', chiefly that it was not only famous 'for a great manufacture of stockings', and for a decisive battle in the Wars of the Roses fought in 1471, but that its 'great old church . . . may indeed be called the largest private church in England'.

Fifty years after Defoe's death the Hon. John Byng, eighteenth-century diarist and inveterate traveller, baited his horse at Tewkesbury before riding on to Malvern Wells. Born in 1742, Byng was a distinguished soldier before gaining his appointment as a Commissioner of Stamps at the age of forty, a post he took up shortly after setting out on the first of the 'tours' that are preserved in his journals. The *Torrington Diaries* – their title is derived from the fact that Byng became the Fifth Viscount Torrington just two weeks before his death, in 1813 – have been described as the 'Rural Rides' of the eighteenth century. Unlike William Cobbett, however, Byng did not set down his observations with publication in mind, and these accounts of his travels only became available to the general reader during the 1930s. Lacking sufficient time to explore the town properly on this occasion, Byng confined himself more or less to a survey of 'the great church which did belong to the abbey. The outside is august,' he recorded, rivalling Defoe in the brevity of his comments, 'but the inside is disfigur'd by ill-built pews.'

Apparently neither Defoe nor Byng seems to have given so much as a thought to William Shakespeare, despite their proximity to Stratford-on-Avon, otherwise they would probably have recalled the line in *Henry IV Part 2* where

Falstaff says of Poins that 'His wit is as thick as Tewkesbury mustard.' In fairness to them, however, as R.P. Beckinsale points out in his *Companion into Gloucestershire* (1939), although 'Shakespeare gave Tewkesbury a reputation for mustard balls, even as early as 1770 no one could remember them ever having been made there.'

* * *

During the spring of 1798 twenty-year-old William Hazlitt embarked on a walking tour from his home in Shropshire, to visit his friend Samuel Taylor Coleridge at Nether Stowey in Somerset. Hazlitt, who, like Coleridge, was a prodigious walker and also something of a troubled genius, became a prolific essayist and a distinguished, though often controversial, political journalist and literary critic. Best remembered, perhaps, for his collection of biographical essays, *The Spirit of the Age* (1825), he was plagued by a chaotic private life and money difficulties until he was eventually reduced to existing in a back room in Soho's Frith Street, where he died in 1830.

These vicissitudes were a thing of the future, however, when Hazlitt strode south from Wem and, after passing through Worcester and Upton-upon-Severn, arrived at Tewkesbury wet through, having been caught in a heavy downpour of rain. He stayed at an inn 'where I sat up all night to read "Paul and Virginia" ', he recalled later in an essay. 'Sweet were the showers in early youth that drenched my body, and sweet the drops of pity that fell upon the books I read!'

Intellectually stimulating though Hazlitt's brush with Saint Pierre's masterpiece must have been for him at Tewkesbury, there was a distinct absence of the *joie de vivre* that accompanied the Pickwickians' excursion there. *The Pickwick Papers*, first issued in twenty monthly parts from April 1836, and in volume form the following year, was written when Charles Dickens was only twenty-five years old. The loosely constructed plot, brimming with bizarre characters and including those now famous visits to Dingley Dell at Christmas and to the Eatanswill parliamentary election, was woven around the adventures of The Pickwick Club, whose chairman was Mr Samuel Pickwick. After an initially lukewarm reception, the novel caught the public's imagination and virtually launched Dickens's immensely successful writing career.

Pickwick, his servant, Sam Weller, and friends, Benjamin Allen and Bob Sawyer, had made quite a day of it by the time they reached The Hop Pole (now The Royal Hop Pole) at Tewkesbury in the evening. They had started out from Bristol early that morning and paused for lunch at The Bell, Berkeley Heath, en route, where their meal was accompanied by an ample supply of bottled ale and Madeira. The party's ultimate destination that day was Birmingham but, at Tewkesbury, as any passer-by may read, even now, from a plaque fixed to the wall by the main entrance of The Royal Hop Pole:

The Hop Pole (now The Royal Hop Pole), Church Street, Tewkesbury, c. 1920s

they stopped to dine; upon which occasion there was more bottled ale, with some more Madeira, and some Port besides . . . Under the influence of these combined stimulants, Pickwick and Mr Ben Allen fell fast asleep for thirty miles, while Bob and Mr Weller sang duets in the dickey.

* * *

It was during the mid-nineteenth century, however, after the novelist Dinah Maria Mulock (later better known as Mrs Craik) visited Tewkesbury, that the town was firmly placed on the literary map. Born at Hartshill near Stoke-on-Trent in 1826, and a contemporary of Charlotte Brontë and George Eliot, Craik was an industrious writer even by Victorian standards. Her first novel, *The Ogilvies*, was published in 1849, and she wrote a further ten in quick succession before *John Halifax, Gentleman* – the only book for which she is remembered today – appeared seven years later. This classic and rather sentimental tale hinges on the rise of a destitute young orphan who, by dint of hard work and high principles, becomes one of Norton Bury's most respected citizens, the eponymous 'gentleman' of the story.

The book was an immense popular success, both in Britain and the United States, from the moment it appeared and continues to be widely read today. Not surprisingly, perhaps, Tewkesbury has become an indispensable port of call for American tourists over the years, many of whom are keen to see at first hand the ancient streets and quaint buildings among which the story of John Halifax's rise by self-improvement was played out.

Craik, too, had first seen the town through a tourist's eyes, while staying with friends at Cheltenham in the early 1850s. Enchanted by the place, she decided to make its close streets, with their overhanging, half-timbered houses set against the backdrop of the old abbey, the heart of the new novel she was planning. Her faithful portrait of Tewkesbury has made it possible for readers of the book ever since to identify the scenery of 'Halifax country'.

Of course, a great deal has altered in the town since those days around the turn of the nineteenth century, when the penniless waif, John Halifax, was given employment and shelter by the Quaker tanner, Abel Fletcher, befriended by Fletcher's delicate son, Phineas, and, later, married to Ursula March in Norton Bury's venerable abbey. Riddled though Tewkesbury still is today with alleys and tight passageways, you would be hard-pressed to find any trace of

the narrow, dirty alley leading to the High Street, [with] open house-doors on either side, through which came the drowsy burr of many a stocking-loom, the prattle of children paddling in the gutter and sailing thereon a fleet of potato parings.

These were the alleys, said Craik in the guise of her narrator, Phineas Fletcher, where you could find 'hundreds of our poor folk living, huddled together in misery, rags, and dirt'.

However, the timber-framed Bell Hotel is still in its old position near the churchyard gates. Craik lunched there on her first visit to Tewkesbury, and was told by the landlady that the building had formerly belonged to a tanner. In that moment, so legend has it, Abel Fletcher's home and trade were born. His business was established at the Abbey Mill by the Avon; later it was christened 'Abel Fletcher's Mill' and the tannery gave way to a restaurant, in which capacity the mill can still be seen and visited today.

Tudor House, in the High Street, from where Ursula March first set eyes on John Halifax as a young beggar-lad, when he arrived at Norton Bury, has since become a hotel, although not before John Moore spent his childhood there, during the early years of the twentieth century. And elegantly overshadowing it all is the same old abbey where Ursula had 'walked quietly up the aisle in her plain white muslin gown' to marry John Halifax, and where today groups of visitors may often be

Abel Fletcher's Mill on the River Avon, Tewkesbury, with the abbey tower rising above the rooftops of the town

found scrutinizing a neo-Renaissance memorial tablet in the south transept. The object of their interest is a medallion profile portrait of Craik, which commemorates her link with the town and is inscribed with a few words from the closing chapters of *John Halifax, Gentleman*:

> Each in his place is fulfilling his day, and passing away, just as that Sun is passing. Only we know not whither he passes: while whither we go we know, and the Way we know – the same yesterday, today, and forever.

* * *

In 1911 E. Temple Thurston hired a canal boat and made a leisurely progress along the waterways of central England. It appears that the spirit of discovery and pure escapism were the driving forces behind the month-long journey which, according to his chronicle of the trip, *The Flower of Gloster*, published later that same year, took him through Tewkesbury, a place, he wrote, full of strange crevices . . . Glance down them and you might almost believe the sixteenth century were back again. Old half-timbered gables lean across the narrow spaces until they well-nigh touch each other . . . I wished then, when once I had seen a little of it, that I had time to see it all. It is so closely written into the pages of England's history that it is a lesson, if it be nothing else.

Temple Thurston, another prolific novelist and a playwright, too, was born in 1879. By the time he embarked on *The Flower of Gloster* his successful career was well under way and enjoying a particularly productive period. He had just published two of his most outstanding novels, both of which are now long forgotten: *The City of Beautiful Nonsense* and *The Greatest Wish in the World*. Perhaps it was because his first marriage had recently ended in divorce, however, that he felt a particular need to escape from it all in the peaceful ambience of England's waterways.

The Tewkesbury of Temple Thurston's day, of course, was the same town that Moore would have recognized. Moore was born there in 1907 and, by the time he died sixty years later, he had become one of England's leading country writers, both as a novelist and through his factual books on country matters. He was a busy journalist and broadcaster, and he also made a wider contribution to literature in general: as a one-time chairman of the Society of Authors, and as a co-founder in 1946 – with his friend, the writer Robert Henriques – of the Cheltenham Festival of Literature, remaining its director for the next ten years.

After his first book – a novel called *Dixon's Cubs* – was published in 1930, Moore resigned from his uncle's firm of auctioneers at Tewkesbury, where he had been working since leaving Malvern College, and set out on his literary career. Over the next few years he was to produce a succession of novels, volumes of short stories and essays, and topographical books, including his lively and provocative *The Cotswolds*, which appeared in 1937. Two years later he published a sensitive and highly readable account of Edward Thomas's life.

Despite such industry on the home front, Moore had gone to Spain in 1936 as a freelance correspondent to cover the Civil War. Then in 1939, at the outbreak of the Second World War, he joined the Royal Navy and became a Fleet Air Arm pilot, an experience that led him to write a book about the service. It was in 1945, however, that he published what is probably his finest novel, *Portrait of Elmbury*, the first part of his 'Brensham' trilogy. *Brensham Village* followed in 1946 and, two years later, *The Blue Field* completed the sequence.

Portrait of Elmbury is a warm, affectionate and only thinly disguised account of Moore's early life at Tewkesbury. Loosely framed by the two world wars, it covers the period when he lived at Tudor House, 'the loveliest house in Elmbury,' he explained, 'which . . . looked out across a wide main street upon the filthiest slum I have ever set eyes on in England'.

Tudor House, High Street, Tewkesbury, c. 1920s

Later, when his father died towards the end of the First World War, the family left Tudor House and Moore was sent to school about ten miles away, but he always came back to Elmbury during the holidays. Then he 'enjoyed a kind of Richard Jefferies boyhood, in which . . . each season had its special delights': birds-nesting at Easter, fishing and butterfly-hunting during the summer, and following the hounds or skating on frozen ponds at Christmas.

The book is laden with vignettes of memorable characters: the 'Hogarthian figure' of Nobbler Price the greengrocer, gin-sodden Black-Sal, and a hot-tempered couple called the Hooks, all residents of Double Alley, the name of the unspeakable slum opposite Tudor House. Then there was the ancient town crier, 'dried-up and perpetually parched; so that between cries he must needs hobble into the nearest pub to wet his desiccated larynx', and, borrowing the names appropriately enough from Shakespeare, there were three good-natured rogues, Pistol, Bardolph and Nym. 'Magistrates and police despaired of them,' recalled Moore. 'And yet there was nothing mean or sordid about their misdemeanours. Sheer mischief and a sort of impishness illuminated all their crimes.'

* * *

If the Norman abbey dominates Tewkesbury at close quarters, then four miles or so north and east of the town, as the crow flies, and just over the border into Hereford and Worcester, Bredon Hill is equally conspicuous in its own way. The 'Stranded Whale', as it is known locally, has a present-day advocate in Fred Archer, whose many books celebrating life on and around Bredon Hill are much-prized by country-lovers everywhere. Archer was born in 1915 at Ashton-under-Hill, to the east of Bredon and just over the border from Gloucestershire. It was, he wrote, 'a land of cider, fat bacon and bread pudding', and his between-the-wars childhood was studded with a whole gallery of colourful characters: the bachelor brother drain-layers Maxim and Tart Middleton; 'Peg

Leg' Stubbins the stone-breaker; 'Thatcher' Buggins, and Bumper Morgan, 'a man who was so rural, such a student of nature, that to have placed him in a city street would have been like putting a cart-horse in the paddock at Ascot'.

Bredon Hill, an outcrop of the Cotswolds, rises to over a thousand feet, and it served as something of a barometer for Elmbury folk in Moore's young day, as he explained in *Brensham Village*:

> Almost every morning of their lives the weather-wise people of Elmbury lift up their eyes to glance at Brensham Hill. According to its clearness or mistiness they make their prognosis of the day; taking into account, of course, the season of the year, the direction of the wind, and the rheumaticky pains in their backs, their legs or their elbows . . . Brensham, therefore, is as much a part of Elmbury's landscape as the great Norman tower of Elmbury Abbey . . . It rises up in front of you as you walk down the wide main street; it appears behind the bowler's arm when you bat on the cricket-field; it is the first landmark of home . . .

Moore's memory is kept green in Tewkesbury today by the Countryside Museum in Church Street, which bears his name. There could hardly be a more fitting tribute to him, especially in the light of Sir Compton MacKenzie's moving obituary, which appeared in *The Times* shortly after Moore's death. 'No writer in these days,' Mackenzie explained, 'when the English countryside is being slowly exterminated to gratify material progress, was able to preserve what is left to it with the eloquent and accurate observation of John Moore.'

CHAPTER FOUR

Country House Society

Gloucestershire is particularly well-endowed with manor houses and country mansions of all shapes and sizes, two fine examples of which, in the north-east corner of the county, immediately spring to mind. The interior of Snowshill is famous for its extraordinary range of contents – from samurai swords to sedan chairs – assembled by the manor's eccentric owner, Charles Wade, during the first half of the twentieth century. In sharp contrast Hidcote Manor, near Mickleton, is noted for its magnificent garden.

At Dumbleton, less than ten miles east of Tewkesbury, where Bredon Hill is just as much a barometer and a part of the landscape as for 'Elmbury folk', the present early nineteenth-century hall, which serves as a holiday and convalescent centre, is now in the hands of the Post Office Fellowship of Remembrance. It stands in seclusion at the end of its winding half-mile drive, set against the backdrop of wooded Dumbleton Hill. It is hard to imagine a more peaceful spot in which to take a well-earned break or recuperate from an illness than this idyllic village, with its assortment of half-timbered thatched cottages, and where the church bells of St Peter's are said, locally, at least, to be the sweetest in Gloucestershire. The hall was built in Tudor style for Edward Holland, who was the MP for West Worcestershire and one of the founders of the Royal Agricultural College at Cirencester. He was also a first cousin of the Victorian novelist and social reformer Mrs Elizabeth Gaskell, so the author of *Cranford* and *North and South* was no stranger to Dumbleton Hall, where she paid regular family visits.

Dumbleton Hall

Born in 1810, Gaskell was brought up in Knutsford, Cheshire (the model for 'Cranford' and, later, for 'Hollingford', in her final, unfinished novel, *Wives and Daughters*). Both the daughter and the wife of Unitarian ministers, she was a tireless campaigner for social reconciliation and used several of her novels, including *Mary Barton* (1848) and *North and South* (1855), as vehicles to encourage a better understanding and greater tolerance between traditionally opposed factions of society: employer and employee, the rich and poor. Inevitably she occasionally attracted controversy, not least in *Ruth* (1853), a novel that sorely inflamed many of her readers by its unfashionably sympathetic treatment of unmarried motherhood.

There are several letters to be found in Gaskell's published correspondence that suggest she was sometimes preoccupied with literary matters while staying at her cousin Edward's home. During a visit in August 1856, for example, her thoughts were obviously dwelling on the biography she was preparing about Charlotte Brontë, the author of *Jane Eyre*, who had died the previous year. Written at the request of Brontë's clergyman father, Gaskell's account of her friend's life was also the subject of some fierce criticism when it appeared, and several supposedly libellous statements were withdrawn from the first edition. Nevertheless, it has long been recognized as one of the finest of English biographies, and is not infrequently mentioned in the same breath as Boswell's *Life of Johnson*.

Gaskell was considering the possible ramifications of her biography being published in 1857, and thus coinciding with the first appearance of Brontë's own heavily autobiographical novel, *The Professor*. She wrote to her publisher and friend, George Smith, from Dumbleton Hall on 15 August 1856:

> I do not myself see there is any occasion to regulate the appearance of 'The Professor' by the appearance of the memoir. It seems to me as if each would possess a strong independent interest. Perhaps you will let me know what you think.

Four days later she wrote to Smith again:

> The Life, will, I think, be ready by Xmas – 240 (of my pages) are ready now. The number of Brontë's pages in 'The Professor' is 340. Her writing is so beautifully even and regular that, from this, I think you could make a good calculation.

In 1864 Gaskell's eldest daughter, Marianne, became officially engaged to Holland's eldest son, Thurstan, after a lengthy, though unacknowledged, attachment between the couple. At first Holland strongly disapproved of the match, mainly on financial grounds: Marianne might have been the daughter of a distinguished novelist, but she was not in any sense an heiress and he had a large family to provide for. Gaskell confided to Smith:

It has been a great deal of worry. [Thurstan's] father objects strongly – has forbidden me and Minny [Marianne] to reply to his letters & I fear he will withdraw his present allowance to his son when he marries . . . We are in the middle of a pretty family tiff, which will, I suppose, die out in time, but it is unpleasant in the interval.

Matters were duly smoothed over just as Gaskell had predicted, and Holland's approval was eventually obtained for Marianne and Thurstan's engagement. Sadly, however, Gaskell died suddenly at the end of 1865, and the couple were not married until the following year.

After Holland's death in 1875, Dumbleton Hall passed into the hands of the Eyres-Monsell family, through one of whose members a future Poet Laureate was to establish a brief connection with the place. When John Betjeman was an undergraduate at Magdalen College, Oxford, during the late 1920s, he became acquainted with Graham Eyres-Monsell through a close mutual friend, Lionel Perry. A visit to Dumbleton Hall followed and, perhaps not surprisingly, Betjeman was moved to write several poems about the house, one of which was composed in mock-Longfellow style and began with a description of the mansion's sheltered situation in the lee of Dumbleton Hill:

Not a farmhouse, not a homestead, only trees on either hand
Billowing like heaps of cushions on the sofa of the land.

This poem, called 'Dumbleton Hall', was discovered by Betjeman's biographer, Bevis Hillier, among some of the late Poet Laureate's previously unpublished material held in the University of Victoria, British Columbia. It found an audience when it was included in Betjeman's *Uncollected Poems*, which appeared in 1982.

By coincidence Perry was also responsible for introducing Betjeman to John Dugdale, whose home at Sezincote, once described as 'a good joke, but a good house, too', a few miles east of Moreton-in-Marsh, was designed in Indian style by the architect Samuel Pepys Cockerell. Built at the beginning of the nineteenth century Sezincote, with its domes and minarets, is an arresting sight as it rises out of the surrounding woodland, and vaguely reminiscent of the Victorian novelist Edward Bulwer-Lytton's rather more self-indulgent creation at Knebworth House in Hertfordshire. 'I have seen Americans and "hikers" goggling with amazement as they caught a glimpse of the mansion while trespassing in the park,' declared Betjeman, writing in a 1931 issue of the *Architectural Review.*

Betjeman, who, unlike many of his friends at Magdalen was neither the son of an aristocratic family nor even a member of the upper-middle class (his father was 'in trade' as a manufacturer of locks and other household items), was a frequent and popular guest at Sezincote during his undergraduate days. As he was to describe thirty years later in his blank-verse autobiography, *Summoned By Bells*, he became exceedingly fond of Dugdale's parents and, in particular, his mother:

> Dear Mrs Dugdale, mother of us all,
> In trailing and Edwardian-looking dress,
> A Sargent portrait in your elegance . . .

These were early days for Betjeman in the elevated world of country house weekends and, with his life-long passion for architecture, it was inevitable that the place should make a considerable impression on him:

> Stately and strange it stood, the Nabob's house,
> Indian without and coolest Greek within,
> Looking from Gloucestershire to Oxfordshire . . .

Evelyn Waugh spent a weekend at Sezincote with Betjeman and the Dugdales during the summer of 1930. He noted in his diary afterwards that the house was 'like Brighton Pavilion only everything in Cotswold stone instead of plaster', adding that it had 'the most lovely view in England'.

Nearby, barely two miles north of Sezincote, stands Batsford Park, a neo-Elizabethan mansion which, in 1886, became the home of the first Lord Redesdale. He was the author of several books, including *Tales of Old Japan*, which was first published in 1871 and is still in print today. The stories, like the arboretum he created at Batsford, which contains a Japanese garden, were inspired by his years on diplomatic service in the Far East.

Writing in a volume of memoirs, Lord Redesdale described how, in 1905, he entertained Edward VII on a visit to Batsford. The king, an enthusiastic gardener himself, was given a conducted tour of the park:

> The next day was taken up with . . . a long drive to Stanway over the Cotswold Hills which I was eager to show him, and so he saw Campden, Broadway and some of the picturesque neighbouring villages . . . The King was very much pleased with this view of a part of his dominions that was new to him . . .

Two of Lord Redesdale's Mitford granddaughters went on to achieve considerable literary reputations for themselves; Nancy as the author of – in addition to other novels and sundry biographies – *Pursuit of Love* (1945) and *Love in a Cold Climate* (1949), while Jessica has published several lively accounts of Mitford family life in *Hons and Rebels* (1960) and *A Fine Old Conflict* (1978).

Writing in her autobiography, *A Life of Contrasts* (1977), a third sister, Diana, recalled the Mitfords' days at Batsford during the First World War, shortly before the property passed out of her family's hands. The Mitford girls and their parents moved into the house after Lord Redesdale's death, in 1916.

She explained:

> Because of the war, and our poverty, we only used a few
> rooms; the rest of the house was in dust sheets . . . We all
> knew that as soon as the war was over Batsford was
> going to be sold because we were too poor to live there.
> We hoped the war would go on forever.

* * *

> At about the same time that Betjeman was taking his
> First steps in learning how to be a guest . . .
> In the large ambience of a country house,

at Sezincote, J.M. Barrie was conducting house parties of his
own in the grand manner over at Stanway, a few miles to the
south-east of Dumbleton. Stanway House, once the summer
residence of the Abbots of Tewkesbury, is the focal point of a
tiny village that, with its gabled cottages of golden Cotswold
stone, has fared better than most in warding off the worst
excesses of the twentieth century, and still retains the air of a
tranquil backwater. It was through his friendship with Lady
Cynthia Asquith, a daughter of the Earl of Wemyss, whose
family had owned Stanway House for centuries, that Barrie
found himself a guest during the Easter holiday of 1921, at this
'fayre manor place', as the early sixteenth-century antiquary,
John Leland, described it. Lady Asquith, whose husband,
Herbert ('Beb'), was not only the son of a former prime
minister but also a poet, acted as Barrie's secretary for nearly
twenty years, and it was her enthusiasm for the old family
home, with its 'restful shabbiness and gentle dilapidation', that
served as the impetus for the famous dramatist's first visit.

Barrie fell in love with Stanway at first sight, 'not only with the
gabled sixteenth-century house,' wrote Lady Asquith in her
biography of him, 'but with its atmosphere which – remote,
cloistered, yet somehow welcoming – seemed, he said, at once to

Stanway House (and church), 'remote, cloistered, yet somehow welcoming . . .'

enfold him like a cloak'. Such was the strength of Barrie's attachment, in fact, that he rented Stanway House for six weeks or so that summer, in an arrangement that suited all parties, and he returned to spend a similar period there every summer until 1932. Thus for a short time each year he became not only the tenant of Stanway House, but also the temporary squire of the village.

Born the son of a hand-loom weaver at Kirriemuir, Tayside, in 1860, and educated at Dumfries Academy and Edinburgh University, Barrie was already in his early sixties by the time he first went to Stanway. He was a distinguished literary figure – not only the famous author of *Peter Pan*, which had first been staged with great success at the Duke of York's Theatre, London, at Christmas in 1904, but also of a string of other plays, including *The Admirable Crichton*, *Quality Street* and *What Every Woman Knows*, all of which had earned him an enviable reputation.

Although his life had been an undeniable triumph professionally, Barrie was always a man of decidedly uncertain temperament: house guests who arrived to find him in sparkling form and engrossed in his twin passions of playing shovelboard indoors or cricket on the Stanway village pitch usually travelled through the doldrums with him as one of his black moods descended and cast a dark shadow over the whole proceedings. 'As always,' wrote Lady Asquith at the end of one Stanway summer, '[Barrie] was fluctuating, unpredictable. Now, he would put others on the best possible terms with themselves; now lower the temperature for miles around.'

Barrie's house guests during each summer's tenancy were usually a mixture of family and friends, and many of those friends were inevitably drawn from the world of literature. Lady Asquith, combining her everyday role as secretary with that of hostess during these annual holidays (Barrie was divorced from his wife), was well-placed to observe the less public side of some of the world's most famous writers during their visits to her parents' country home. Her diaries and letters of the period, which she drew from liberally in her *Portrait of Barrie*, published in 1954, are packed with tantalizing glimpses of some illustrious personalities.

The novelist John Galsworthy, for example, was a regular guest, whose 'almost portentously good manners' Lady Asquith found somewhat daunting at first. 'Upright, correct, immaculately dressed; he looks the very personification of integrity, rectitude, "good form",' was how she described the author of *The Forsyte Saga* in 1925. On later visits, however (to use one of Barrie's least-favourite phrases), he 'grew upon' her. 'I liked his compassion and scrupulous fair-mindedness,' she wrote.

Other Stanway 'regulars' included G.K. Chesterton, 'a delight to everyone' and the inventor of that durable Roman Catholic priest-cum-sleuth, Father Brown; Sir Arthur Conan Doyle, 'burly, unpretentious, lovable, ingenuous', who in Sherlock Holmes created probably the world's most famous amateur detective; and Walter De La Mare, 'the most undisappointing poet that's ever been', according to Lady Asquith, but sorely underrated today. 'I don't believe even the veriest dolt could be one moment in his company,' she added, 'without realizing how different he is from everyone else.' The annual guest lists, as Lady Asquith herself admitted, 'read like scores of items out of "Who's Who" ': L.P. Hartley, George Moore, A.P. Herbert, Harley Granville-Barker, H.G. Wells and many others.

Regardless of who they were, however, guests were co-opted by their host on to cricket teams or to play croquet matches, and sometimes to make up a party with Barrie to visit one of his favourite local villages: Bibury, perhaps, or Stanton, where it became almost an institution for Barrie's guests to take tea with the redoubtable Eliza Wedgwood, great-granddaughter of the famous potter.

On a literary note, Barrie's link with Stanway rests on the great oriel window at the front of the house, which can be seen to some advantage from the adjacent churchyard of St Peter's and which, with its innumerable latticed panes, found a place in *Farewell, Miss Julie Logan*. It is still as much of an attraction to visitors as it ever was. Barrie wrote:

> The great bow window is said by travelled persons to stand alone among windows, for it is twenty-eight feet in height, and more than half as wide. All who come to look at it count its little lozens, as we call the panes, which are to the number of two hundred and sixteen.

The summer of 1932 was Barrie's last at Stanway House; by then he was over seventy and his health was gradually deteriorating. 'This year,' Lady Asquith recorded at the beginning of September, 'I must, alas, admit that I'm glad the last day has come. It has been such a strain that we're all exhausted.' Reading between the lines, it would seem that Barrie's temperament had, perhaps, been at its most unpredictable. However, he left behind not only a useful but also a characteristically generous reminder of the days he had

Thatched cricket pavilion, J.M. Barrie's gift to Stanway

spent in the village. An old railway carriage was serving as the local cricket club pavilion when Barrie first arrived, but, ever the keen cricketer, he replaced it in 1925 with the present attractively thatched building of his own design, which stands beside the village pitch on white staddle-stones. It is a gift that has brought endless pleasure to generations of players and spectators alike over the years.

Barrie died in 1937 but, almost half a century later, while visiting Stanway during the cricket season, Winifred Foley encountered a time-honoured scene being played out in the shadow of that same old pavilion, and one that would have been instantly recognizable to the famous author of *Peter Pan*. She fondly explained:

Wives and children shelter from the heat beneath walnut and pear trees, and prepare tea for the players. Old men in faded straw hats, clenching their pipes in unsafe dentures, mutter about the heroes of the past. Rustic England at its best.

CHAPTER FIVE

Around Dover's Hill

The Cotswold Way long-distance footpath runs in an unbroken line for ninety-five miles, following for most of its length the high continuous edge of the scarp from Bath to Chipping Campden. Opened in 1970, although conceived several decades earlier, it winds through Stanway before meandering on north and east to reach its final destination at the northern tip of the Cotswolds. On its journey from Stanton to Broadway the route bypasses Buckland, a picturesque and straggling hamlet that became Mrs Delany's home in 1715.

Mrs Delany, or Mary Granville as she was known at the time, lived for a while at the manor, which she called 'The Farm', and which is nowadays a restaurant and country house hotel. Her *Autobiography and Correspondence*, published for the first time in the early 1860s, contains a spirited account of her journey to Buckland from London. Her family had left the capital hurriedly and in some danger of arrest as they were out of favour with the Court.

In later life Delany became a friend of Jonathan Swift and Fanny Burney, and she was also a noted 'Blue Stocking' – a member of that large, informal circle of intellectual women, who met at each other's houses in London primarily to enjoy good conversation. As a young woman living in eighteenth-century rural Gloucestershire, however, she found life something of a trial at first. 'I lamented the loss of my young companions, and the universal gaiety I parted with when I left London,' she wrote later, 'and to make the change appear still more gloomy, all this I quitted in November.' But her heart grew lighter with the onset of spring. 'The front of the house faces the finest vale in England, the Vale of Evesham,' she enthused. 'Nothing could be more fragrant and rural: the sheep and cows come bleating and lowing to the pales of the garden.' Matters improved still further with the arrival of an attractive young man called Roberto. The pair duly fell in love, but were unable to marry as Roberto was rich and Mary was poor. Thus Roberto 'withered away and "died for love" ', while Mary sensibly married somebody else!

A mile outside Chipping Campden, as many a footsore long-distance walker will testify, the Cotswold Way arrives at what is now known as Dover's Hill, the setting for the 'Cotswold Olympicks', which, although of uncertain origin, probably hark back to the medieval wakes and feasts once so common in the area. They were revived by Captain Robert Dover in around 1612 and held every year at Whitsun. Dover, a Norfolk man by birth, went to live at Saintbury near Weston-sub-Edge, probably in 1611, and he organized the games with the help of his friend the courtier poet Endymion Porter, who was born at nearby Mickleton. A friend and patron of many poets and painters in his time, Porter was favoured as groom to the royal bedchamber of Charles I, on whose side he fought in the Civil War, and for which he paid the high price of dying abroad in poverty in the changed political climate of later days.

Events at the 'Cotswold Olympicks' included horse-racing, wrestling, sword-fighting, hare-coursing and a variety of other robust activities that subsequently caused the Puritans to frown on them. As a result the games were closed after Dover's death in 1652, but were later revived once more and continued until the early 1850s, when they were stopped by a combination of enclosures and the mayhem that ensued when vast numbers of people – mainly gangs of rowdy navvies, who were working at that time on the tunnel destined to carry the Oxford, Worcester and Wolverhampton Railway under Mickleton Hill – flocked in from the surrounding area. The games were resumed in the

1960s and Dover's Hill, more than 180 acres of exposed natural amphitheatre with a panoramic view over the Vale of Evesham, is now owned by the National Trust.

In their heyday the 'Cotswold Olympicks' attracted a great deal of attention from literary folk, not least, perhaps, William Shakespeare himself. There is, for example, that much quoted line from *The Merry Wives of Windsor*: 'How does your fallow greyhound sir?', Master Slender enquires of George Page. 'I heard say he was outrun on Cotsall.' As this play was probably written in around 1596 or 1597, Shakespeare was no doubt familiar with the games in some form or other before Dover took a hand in them. It would seem likely that he had friends and possibly distant family connections in that part of Gloucestershire, which was, after all, very close to his own home at Stratford-on-Avon.

Michael Drayton, the Warwickshire-born poet, whose great topographical poem about England, 'Poly-Olbion', appeared

Dover's Hill, near Chipping Campden, a natural amphitheatre

between 1612 and 1622, was one of thirty-four contributors to *Annalia Dubrensia*, a collection of poems celebrating Dover's 'Olympicks', which was published in 1636. In 'Poly-Olbion' Drayton wrote about the 'Cotswold Olympicks' as they had been in the time before Dover rescued them:

> The Shepherds King
> Whose flock hath chanc'd that yeere the earliest
>   lamb to bring
> In his gay bawdrick sits at his low grassie bord,
> With flawns, curds, clotted creame, and countrie
>   dainties stor'd . . .

Annalia Dubrensia also included offerings from Thomas Heywood and Ben Jonson, among many minor poets of the day now, perhaps deservedly, long forgotten. Taken together the poems tend to be repetitious and mostly unmemorable, but it is worth quoting Jonson's epigram, which provides a neat comment on the climate of the day:

> I cannot bring my Muse to dropp vies
> Twixt Cotswold and the Olimpicke exercise:
> But I can tell thee Dover how thy Games
> Renew the Glories of our Blessed Jeames:
> How they doe keepe alive his memorie,
> With the Glad Countrey and Posteritie:
> How they advance true love and neighbourhood,
> And doe both Church and Common-wealth the good,
> In spite of Hipocrites, who are the worst
> Of subjects. Let such envie till they burst!

That undeservedly little-known work, *The Spiritual Quixote*, written by Richard Graves, an eighteenth-century squire and antiquary of Mickleton, was published in 1772. It relates the adventures of two travellers who set out on the eve of one Whitsuntide intent on saving souls. The first exploit of the book's hero, the reforming Methodist Geoffry Wildgoose, and of his travelling companion, Jerry Tugwell, in this picaresque tale, which came in the wake of Smollett's *Humphry Clinker* and Fielding's *Tom Jones*, actually concerned the 'Cotswold Olympicks', where the pair were eventually forced to concede that discretion is the better part of valour. Approaching Dover's Hill,

> their ears were saluted with a confused noise of drums, trumpets and whistle-pipes . . . There was a great number of swains in their holiday-clothes, with their belts and silk handkerchiefs; and nymphs in straw hats and tawdry ribbands, flaunting, ogling, and coquetting in their rustic way . . .

Wildgoose berated the crowd for spending a religious festival in such a profane manner:

> It was appointed to commemorate the most solemn event recorded in the annals of our religion, namely the effusion of the Holy Spirit upon our primitive apostles. But instead of being filled with the Holy Spirit, as the apostles were, you are filling yourselves with spirituous liquors and strong drink. Oh! my brethren, consider what you are about . . . The very purpose and intent of this ungodly meeting is directly opposite to your most solemn vow at your baptism.

But he failed dismally to gauge the holiday mood of his audience and was forced to beat a hasty retreat, with Tugwell, under a torrent of rotting vegetables and clods of horse dung.

The lane skirting the west of Dover's Hill runs down to Weston-sub-Edge, a pretty, straggling village set against a backdrop of the Cotswold scarp to which, in or around 1696, came that indomitable seventeenth-century traveller, Celia Fiennes. Born in 1662 at Newton Toney near Salisbury, very little is known about her life beyond the few snippets recorded in her journal, which was first published in 1888 as *Through England on a Side Saddle in the Time of William and Mary*, a lively account of her travels through every English county between 1685 and 1703. She passed through Gloucestershire on several occasions, this time calling on her cousin, Pheramus Fiennes, at his parsonage home, 'a neate building all stone,' she recorded, 'and the walls round court gardens and yards are all of stone'. After leaving Weston-sub-Edge behind, Fiennes climbed 'up a vast stony high hazardous hill of neare two mile long', as she later described it, to the summit of Dover's Hill, from where she marvelled at the view, then rode down through Chipping Campden on her way back to London.

* * *

Barely a mile to the north of Dover's Hill lies Aston Subedge, where the largely seventeenth-century manor house was once Porter's home. Close by, and adjoining the village, can be found the estate of Burnt Norton, a place of no small significance in the annals of twentieth-century literature.

The original house at Burnt Norton was built in 1620 by Lord Saye and Sele, Fiennes's grandfather, and was something like a farmhouse in its appearance. At the beginning of the eighteenth century the property came into the hands of the Keyt family, who built a new large mansion next door to the old house. Graves, writing in *The Spiritual Quixote*, described it as having 'very extensive gardens laid out in the expensive taste of the age'. However, the fortunes of the Keyts declined to such an extent that, in 1741, the profligate, alcoholic and insane Sir William Keyt set fire to the house and burned himself to death in the ensuing blaze. The original farmhouse-type building was untouched and is now owned by the Seventh Earl of Harrowby.

Burnt Norton, Aston Subedge, an engraving of the mansion destroyed by fire in 1741

In 1934 the poet T.S. Eliot visited the gardens of the Burnt Norton estate. Eliot, who was born at St Louis, Missouri, in 1888, had already been settled in London for some years and was a well-established and major figure on the English literary scene by that time. His first volume of poetry, which included 'The Love Song of J. Alfred Prufrock', had appeared in 1917, and more recent years had seen the publication of 'The Hollow Men', 'The Journey of the Magi' and 'Ash-Wednesday'.

In 1934 Eliot was staying at Chipping Campden with some relations of Emily Hale, a young American friend who came to England for several summers during the 1930s. Feeling very much at ease in her aunt and uncle's company, Eliot visited Hale quite often and the pair frequently went out for long walks together from Chipping Campden. Eliot wrote about one such excursion in a comic poem called 'A Country Walk: An Epistle to Miss E—— H—— with the humble compliments of her obliged servant, the Author.' This deals with Eliot's terror of cows, and on her copy of the poem Hale wrote, 'We often took long walks in the country about Gloucestershire.' It was left to the gardens of Burnt Norton, however, to provide Eliot with the inspiration and much of the imagery for what would eventually become the first part of his *Four Quartets*.

Following in the wake of his great dramatic success, *Murder in the Cathedral*, 'Burnt Norton', with its enigmatic opening lines:

> Time present and time past
> Are both perhaps present in time future
> And time future contained in time past . . .

was Eliot's first major poem since 'Ash-Wednesday'. It was originally published separately in 1936, and appeared with 'East Coker', 'The Dry Salvages' and 'Little Gidding' to comprise the *Four Quartets* in 1943. Representing the four seasons and the four elements, the poems reached a wide and appreciative audience.

* * *

J.B. Priestley, the Yorkshire-born novelist, playwright and critic, passed through Chipping Campden in the early 1930s in the course of his *English Journey*, when he travelled from the south coast to Tyneside, taking the pulse of a country that was just emerging from the grip of a severe economic depression. Priestley, a native of Bradford, was forty, and had already written *The Good Companions* and *Angel Pavement* by the time *English Journey* appeared in 1934. Clearly the Cotswolds presented him with a welcome contrast to the industrial conurbations that he visited along the way:

> One moved mysteriously through a world of wet gold. The little valleys were as remote as Alallon. The villages arrived like news from another planet. We might have been journeying through the England of the poets, a country made out of men's visions.

When Priestley reached Chipping Campden at last, he found it 'full and fair in the sunlight'.

It was at this unlikely spot – 'Camden Town', as Fiennes once rather confusingly called it, and a place, according to C. Henry Warren, where 'the chain of life' has never been broken – that a young John Masefield, twenty-five years of age and already the author of *Salt-Water Ballads* – containing perhaps his most widely known poem, 'Sea Fever' – first discovered the true power of the theatre and was, indirectly, launched on his own subsidiary career as a playwright. In January 1903 he was invited to Chipping Campden to see a production of Jonson's *The New Inn*, given by members of the Guild of Handicraft. This was a group formed by the architect C.R. Ashbee in the wake of William Morris's Arts and Crafts Movement, and established at Chipping Campden in 1902, after moving away from the East End of London. Masefield was immediately captivated by a play that depended not on scenery or stage 'business' for its impact, but on the speaking of verse poetically, and it set him thinking seriously about writing verse-dramas of his own.

It was to be another four years, however, before Masefield's first play was staged. In the meantime he wrote several prose-dramas, which were not published until much later, and he paid another visit to Chipping Campden and his friends the Ashbees in 1905. He had grown to love the small Cotswold town so dearly that, when the time came to leave on this occasion and return to his London flat, he was moved to express his feelings in verse:

> When I from Campden town depart
> I leave my wits, I lose my art,
> A melancholy clouds my face
> I feel as though I fell from grace . . .

During the spring of 1906, Masefield was approached by the actor and director, Harley Granville-Barker, who was enjoying a highly successful period at The Court Theatre in London, to advise on the use of sea shanties in a production he was mounting of Shaw's play, *Captain Brassbound's Conversion*. Possibly this direct contact with the theatre at such a lively and innovative time in The Court's history gave Masefield just the impetus he required, and his play *The Campden Wonder* was produced at the theatre the following February. Based on a true story – a miscarriage of justice that had occurred in seventeenth-century Chipping Campden – Granville-Barker's production was not particularly well received. When *The Tragedy of Nan* was staged the following year, however, a play that Masefield set on the banks of the Severn, at Broadoak, audiences and critics alike were much more enthusiastic, and the piece was immediately revived at the Haymarket Theatre following its initial run at The Court.

Masefield went on to write other plays for the professional theatre, but he also developed a keen interest in amateur dramatics. During the 1920s, when the Masefields lived at Boar's Hill, a distinctly literary-minded suburb of Oxford, they mounted many high-quality local productions with a company called the Hill Players, whose vice-presidents included John Galsworthy and John Drinkwater. Performances were given in a small theatre called the 'Music Room', which was built next door to the Masefields' home, Hill Crest. The whole project was the realization of an ambition that Masefield had formed on that January evening in 1903 at Chipping Campden.

* * *

It would be impossible to leave this quiet corner of Gloucestershire without paying a visit to the village, three miles east of Stow-on-the-Wold, whose name must be familiar to many generations of schoolchildren. It was a place that was memorably captured for ever at a particular moment in its history by the poet Edward Thomas, whose train made a brief but unscheduled stop at Adlestrop while carrying him to see the Frosts at Leddington on a fine June day in 1914.

Jane Austen had been an occasional visitor to the village rectory, later called Adlestrop House, at the beginning of the nineteenth century. It was the home of her mother's cousin, the Reverend Thomas Leigh. A younger member of the family, Chandos Leigh, who was born in 1792 and lived for most of his life at Adlestrop, apparently made something of a name for himself as a poet, although his is clearly a reputation which has not endured. F.E. Witts, the nineteenth-century Cotswold parson and diarist, described him as 'an eccentric mortal . . . a poet in a small way', adding enigmatically that 'one of his earlier productions, "The Pleasures of Love" was, by the prudence of his friends, suppressed'.

The Leighs had owned Adlestrop Park since the sixteenth century, and it is possible that Austen drew on her own recollections of the mansion in her description of the fictitious Northanger Abbey. In the absence of any firm evidence from the author herself, however, it can remain no more than informed speculation, based on the fact that Austen began writing her novel of that name in 1798, at a time when she would probably have been most familiar with the rectory and its surroundings.

Thus Adlestrop undeniably owes its celebrity to Thomas alone and one feels that, in a sense, the village, wrapped in its gentle undulations, had been waiting all its days just for that moment when the poet's train would draw up there unexpectedly at the humble little station. The brief, spare poem, which exquisitely captures the atmosphere of a rural England whose tranquillity would soon be irrevocably shattered by the First World War, was actually written some months after that war had begun, Thomas merely making a short note of the incident in his diary on 23rd June: 'Then we stopped at Adlestrop, through the windows could be heard a chain of blackbirds' songs at 12.45 and one thrush and no man

An unscheduled stop at Adlestrop station led to Edward Thomas's famous poem

seen, only a hiss of engine letting off steam.' In that entry, though, was the germ of his best-known poem, with its famous opening stanza:

> Yes, I remember Adlestrop –
> The name, because one afternoon
> Of heat the express-train drew up there
> Unwontedly. It was late June.

The author Susan Hill, writing in her book *The Spirit of the Cotswolds* (1988), says that she deliberately avoids Adlestrop whenever travelling in the area, preferring not to disturb her personal vision of the village – derived from her love for Thomas's poem – with what she might find there. Three-quarters-of-a-century have elapsed since Thomas passed through, and the years have certainly wrought some changes. Trains no longer stop at Adlestrop because the station is closed, axed in the Beeching cuts, although the main line from

Paddington to Worcester passes close by. Somewhat incongruously the old platform sign now graces the village bus-shelter, situated at the foot of the hill that runs up past the tiny thatched post office and curves round to the church of St Mary Magdalene. Otherwise this delightful village of golden stone houses and cottages is surprisingly little-changed since Thomas's day, except that it is now known to millions of poetry-lovers all over the world and possesses one of the most famous place-names in the whole of Gloucestershire.

CHAPTER SIX

Towards 'A Cotswold Village'

The journey southwards from Adlestrop, hugging the border with Oxfordshire to the east, takes the traveller through countryside dotted here and there with villages and hamlets that truly nestle in the gentle, undulating landscape. Any number of these small communities could be the prototype for J.B. Priestley's 'Hitherton-on-the-Wole', in that glorious theatrical romp through England, *The Good Companions*.

The imaginary Hitherton was the Cotswold home of Miss Trant, the colonel's daughter. It was a village almost equidistant from Chipping Campden to the north, Cirencester to the south, Burford to the east and Cheltenham to the west. A glance at a map suggests Bourton-on-the-Water as a possible contender, from a geographical point of view at least, although I feel it should more properly be Stow-on-the-Wold. But doubtless Priestley's 'Hitherton' is an amalgam of several such places all rolled into one. He wrote:

> Sometimes motorists, hurrying from lunch at Oxford to tea at Broadway or Chipping Campden, lose their way and find themselves at Hitherton . . . There are some days, however, when people do not lose their way and find themselves in Hitherton, but deliberately go there and stay there.

It was from Hitherton, after her father's death, that Miss Trant set off on the holiday that would lead to her once-in-a-lifetime sojourn with Jerry Jerningham, Inigo Jollifant, Jess Oakroyd and the other larger-than-life characters who comprised the travelling theatrical troupe, 'The Good Companions', an adventure that was to result in her marriage to Dr McFarlane. It was a Monday morning in September as she drove away to embark on that fateful trip, and 'went rolling down the hill, eastward out of Hitherton . . . The valley lay all golden in the deep sunshine, the morning was as crisp as a nut'.

Priestley fell in love with the Cotswolds, 'the most English and the least spoiled of our countrysides', as he described them in the 1930s, and was particularly captivated by the old buildings fashioned out of local stone. 'Villages, manor houses, farmsteads, built of such magical material,' he enthused during his *English Journey*, with The Slaughters in mind, 'do not merely keep on existing but live like noble lines of verse, lighting up the mind that perceives them.'

He was, of course, not the only traveller to have been impressed by this corner of Gloucestershire, although when the Hon. John Byng passed through Northleach in June 1784, on his tour from London to North Wales and back, he was slightly less than enthusiastic about the area. 'Northleach,' he recorded, 'is a poor dismal place, built of stone that turns black; and gives a very monastic look.' Perhaps the bad weather he was experiencing caused him to see with something of a jaundiced eye, for it had started raining very heavily soon after he passed through Burford. At The King's Head, one of Northleach's former coaching inns, he had dined 'on good, hot pigeon pye. I mention hot,' he emphasized, 'because the weather is so damp, & cold, as to appear October'.

In contrast the antiquary John Leland seems to have been less difficult to please, according to his *Itinerary through England and Wales*, which was first published in around 1710. To him 'Northlech [sic]' was simply 'a praty, uplandish toune', as indeed was Fairford, which he described in precisely the same terms.

Byng visited Fairford, too, in July 1787, entering Gloucestershire on that occasion by way of St John's Bridge at

Lechlade, 'a small market town,' he noted in his diary, 'with nothing of curiosity in, or about it'. Just under thirty years later, however, in 1815, all that was to change when the poet Percy Bysshe Shelley rowed up the Thames from Old Windsor to Lechlade with his young mistress, Mary Godwin, who soon afterwards became not only the poet's wife, but also a famous author in her own right, as the creator of 'Frankenstein'. They were accompanied by Thomas Love Peacock, whose satirical novels *Headlong Hall* and *Nightmare Abbey* parodied the contemporary vogue for Gothic fiction. Having fallen in with, and then decided against, Shelley's original plan to row to the source of the Thames at Coates, they stayed the night at a local inn, where Shelley enjoyed 'three mutton chops, well peppered', and then rode back to Old Windsor the following day. His poem 'A Summer Evening Churchyard' was inspired by, and probably largely written during, this brief visit, and a stone placed in the churchyard wall during the late 1960s – at the beginning of what is now known as Shelley's Walk – quotes some lines from the poem, as a permanent reminder of the occasion: 'Here could I hope . . . that death did hide from human sight sweet secrets.'

Fairford, just four miles west of Lechlade, is perhaps best known as the birthplace, in April 1792, of John Keble, author of *The Christian Year*. The Keble family originally came from Suffolk, but settled in Gloucestershire during the sixteenth century. Keble's father became the vicar of Coln St Aldwyns, one of Fairford's neighbouring parishes, and, after his own ordination in 1816, John Keble assisted his father there.

Later, in 1823, Keble – after leading an academic life for a few years as a tutor at Oriel College, Oxford – was appointed to a curacy at Southrop near Fairford, being responsible at the same time for the two small churches in the twin villages of Eastleach Turville and Eastleach Martin nearby. Standing on either side of the River Leach, the churches are linked by an old clapper bridge, called Keble's Bridge, but only St Andrew's

Keble's Bridge, spanning the River Leach at Eastleach Turville

at Turville is still in use. Then, in 1826, he returned to live in Fairford, from where he acted as curate at Coln St Aldwyns until his father's death nine years later.

The Christian Year, Keble's volume of sacred verse for Sundays and holidays throughout the year, was published anonymously in 1827 and enjoyed an immediate and wide success. A second volume, *Lyra Innocentium*, which appeared almost twenty years later, proved rather less popular. *The Christian Year* did much to assist Keble's election as Professor of Poetry at Oxford, during the winter of 1831, at a time when he was also engaged in preparing a complete edition of the works of the sixteenth-century theologian Richard Hooker. Deeply intellectual, although personally unambitious, Keble spent the last thirty years of his life as vicar of the country parish of Hursley, near Winchester, in Hampshire.

'Fairford', wrote Leland, 'never flourished afore ye Tames came to it' (in a reference to the family and not the river!). 'John

Tame began the fair new chirche of Fairforde,' he explained, 'and Edward Tame finished it.' St Mary's, one of the great Cotswold wool churches, was built between 1490 and 1530, and its magnificent sequence of stained-glass windows, depicting the Bible story from the Creation to the Crucifixion, has made it justly famous throughout the world. Byng made a minute inspection of these windows while he was staying in the town:

> They contain much history of the Old and New Testaments, the portraits of the Apostles, of Roman Emperors, saints &c &c; and particularly a ludicrous representation of the Day of Judgement. (A woman driven to Hell in a wheelbarrow). They are charmingly colour'd, and well preserved by wire lattices.

Afterwards he returned to his inn, The Bull, for 'a good dinner of trout, and cold boil'd beef rowl'd up as tho collar'd'.

Even that waspish old political agitator, William Cobbett, of whom it was once said that he made politics his religion rather than religion his politics, called St Mary's 'one of the prettiest churches in the kingdom' when he passed through Fairford on a 'Rural Ride' in the autumn of 1826. In characteristically acerbic style he reflected:

> One is naturally surprised to see that its windows of beautiful stained glass had the luck to escape not only the fangs of the ferocious 'good Queen Bess'; not only the unsparing plundering minions of James I; but even the devastating ruffians of Cromwell.

* * *

Ablington lies roughly five miles north-west of Fairford and stands, like that town, on the banks of the River Coln, forming the northern point of a triangle completed by Cirencester, seven miles to the south-west. It is less than a mile, however, from neighbouring and much-visited Bibury, one of the most beautiful villages in England according to William Morris, the nineteenth-century writer, painter and craftsman whose home at Kelmscott, although in Oxfordshire, was only a short distance away. Few visitors who have ambled past that long terrace of steeply gabled, seventeenth-century weavers' cottages known as Arlington Row (the buildings themselves are converted from a much older sheephouse) would dream of contradicting that Victorian arbiter of taste and founder, in 1877, of the Society for the Protection of Ancient Buildings. On a more prosaic note it was at Bibury that Byng enjoyed two basins of that noisome delicacy, snail tea, with his breakfast one morning, claiming that it was 'always of sovereign use' to his lungs.

Ablington, however, although merely a hamlet, has become famous in its own right, for it was to the sixteenth-century Ablington Manor, a majestic gabled building of grey Cotswold stone, which stands close to the road yet is half hidden from view behind a high wall, that J. Arthur Gibbs went to live just

Ablington Manor

over a hundred years ago, and where he wrote his classic book about the countryside, *A Cotswold Village*. This was first published in 1898, shortly before his tragically early death.

Gibbs was born in Westminster in 1867, into a wealthy family of Somerset origin, and was educated at Eton. His great love for the Cotswolds developed when he became an undergraduate at Christ Church, Oxford. Within a few years of leaving university he was installed at Ablington Manor as the squire of the village. A young man in his mid-twenties, he possessed towards his dependant neighbours an attitude that was at the same time conventional and benevolent, yet this was also an approach that would be guaranteed to send a frisson down most spines today, with its undisguised air of forthright patronage.

For all Gibbs's genuine concern about farm labourers' appalling living conditions and their need to support often large families on pitifully low wages, many of the attitudes evinced in his book are now, inevitably, hopelessly dated. In a typical passage he wrote:

> The Cotswold people are like their country, healthy, bright, clean, and old-fashioned; and the more educated and refined a man may happen to be, the more in touch he will be with them – not because the peasants are educated and refined, so much as because they are not half-educated and half-refined, but simple, honest, god-fearing folk, who mind their own business and have not sought out many inventions. I am referring now to labourers . . . A primitive people, as often as not they are 'nature's gentlemen'. . .

Elsewhere he speaks of 'extraordinary honesty' being 'a very marked characteristic of the village peasant', and the sleep of the labouring man being sweet.

At the same time Gibbs was filled with genuine respect for the particular skills that the country people possessed. 'To watch a boy of 14 years,' he wrote, with obvious admiration, 'managing a couple of great strong cart-horses, either at the plough or with the waggons, is a sight to gladden the heart of man.' And he genuinely relished the idiosyncrasies of the many old 'characters' who came his way, including his own carter, whom he described as 'a kind of hero' for having twenty-one children by the same wife! By all contemporary accounts Gibbs seems to have been a much-loved and conscientious squire, who had the welfare of his tenants very much at heart.

The real strength of *A Cotswold Village*, however, lies in its passages of glorious prose, making it a yardstick against which to measure the outpouring of Cotswold literature that has appeared over the course of this century. Gibbs's description of his first glimpse of Ablington, for example, a village 'not a hundred miles from London, yet "far from the madding crowd's ignoble strife" ', has an almost other-worldly quality about it:

> One fine September evening, having left all traces of railways and the ancient Roman town of Cirencester some seven long miles behind me, with wearied limbs I sought this quiet, sequestered spot. Suddenly, as I was wondering how amid these never ending hills there could be such a place as I had been told existed, I beheld it at my feet, surpassing beautiful! Below me was a small village, nestling amid a wealth of stately trees. The hand of man seemed in some bygone time to have done all that was necessary to render the place habitable, but no more.

Gibbs would be pleasantly surprised, I think, at how little the village has altered over the years.

Sadly Gibbs did not live long enough to enjoy the fruits of his literary success. When *A Cotswold Village* was reviewed in *The Times* in January 1899, some mention was made of the author's 'scholarly touch and . . . pretty taste for letters', but there were to be no more books from Gibbs. He died from a heart attack just four months later, aged only thirty-one.

CHAPTER SEVEN

An Arcadian Place

Writing in his book *The Cotswolds* during the late 1930s, John Moore gave it as his, somewhat controversial, opinion that Cirencester possessed not only the largest country houses, the best polo ponies and the most expensive cars, but also 'the dullest society and the most extravagant young women in Gloucestershire. It is even now as it was in Roman times,' he added provocatively, 'around Corinium Dobunorum rich men flourish like weeds.' As Moore suggests, in his inimitable fashion, Cirencester has enjoyed a decidedly prosperous history, and today this bustling south Gloucestershire market town of nearly seventeen thousand souls is still a busy crossroads for two major routes – the Foss Way and the Ermin Way – a reminder of the time when, in Roman Britain, Cirencester was the second largest town in the country, after London.

John Byng spent a night in Cirencester, in a 'miserable, old, cold inn', having taken the shortest route on horseback from Fairford, directing his steps through Ampney St Peter and Ampney Crucis. After dining, and then drinking a 'praiseworthy' pint of port wine, he took himself off to inspect the parish church of St John the Baptist. 'The steeple is very grand and lofty,' he recorded, adding that the interior of the building was 'abundant of old chapels, brasses and tombs'.

St John's, which stands in the Market Place, was originally built as a small parish church, then enlarged to cathedral-like proportions a few centuries later in the days of Cirencester's supremacy as a wool market. From the top of the 132 ft church tower it is possible to get a clear view over Lord Bathurst's estate, Cirencester Park, lying to the north-west of the town. Byng ventured there from his inn in a post-chaise but, deciding that it would take at least three days to survey properly, he contented himself with little more than a cursory glance and wrote of it a touch dismissively as 'all avenues or small pitiful clumps . . . Avenue upon avenue, and cut upon cut – all straight and formal, with numbers of temples, Gothic buildings &c'. In *A Cotswold Year* C. Henry Warren described the park as 'a sort of English imitation of Versailles and to walk in it is to slip into the eighteenth century without an effort'.

The thirty thousand acre park, which is open to the public throughout the year, was the brainchild of Allen, the First Earl Bathurst, who was born in 1684 and lived to be over ninety. He was acquainted with some of the greatest literary figures of his age, including John Gay, William Congreve and Laurence Sterne. It was the author of *Tristram Shandy*, in fact, who described the aged earl, then over eighty, as a 'prodigy', with 'all the wit and promptness of a man of thirty; a disposition to be pleased, and a power to please others beyond whatever I knew; added to which a man of learning, courtesy and feeling'.

It fell to the poet Alexander Pope, however, who shared Earl Bathurst's enthusiasm for landscape gardening, to assist with the design of Cirencester Park. The result was a geometrical confection of woodlands and grassy rides, studded with a number of eye-catching garden follies, including the famous Pope's Seat, an ornamental shelter where the diminutive poet – barely four-and-a-half feet tall, after his growth had been arrested by a childhood illness – is said to have composed his verse. Entering this bower while walking in Cirencester Park one day, Warren recalled how he had half expected to find Pope himself reclining there, scribbling away merrily. Instead he found it occupied 'by a short and bristly grey-haired man, sitting on the seat and eating his sandwiches. "Queer old place,

Pope's Seat, Cirencester Park

isn't it?", he asked nervously, ill at ease, as if he too had been surprised in his eighteenth century reverie,' explained Warren. ' "And they were queer old boys," he added, "some of those poets." '

Pope was a regular visitor to Cirencester Park for at least a part of many summers from 1715 onwards. He wrote:

> I look upon myself as the magician appropriated to the place, without whom no mortal can penetrate into the recesses of those sacred shades. I could pass whole days in only describing the future and as yet visionary beauties that are to rise in these scenes: the place that is to be built, the pavilions that are to glitter, the colonnades that are to adorn them.

In 1726 Pope was joined at Cirencester Park by his friend, the Anglo-Irish poet and satirist Jonathan Swift, the latter, it was said, bearing with him the manuscript of *Gulliver's Travels*, which was published that same year. In the temporary absence of Earl Bathurst the two men lodged at the home of a tenant farmer, in a cottage that, according to Mrs Delany who saw it some time later, 'burst with pride . . . after entertaining so illustrious a person' as Swift and had to be rebuilt!

Pope was moved to address his third moral essay, 'Of the Use of Riches', to Earl Bathurst, partly as a result of the good sense demonstrated by that great Gloucestershire landowner in the disposal of his wealth:

> Oh teach us, Bathurst, yet unspoiled with wealth,
> That secret rare between the extremes to move
> Of mad good-nature and of mean self-love.

Four years later, however, in 1737, the poet protested, in the second book of his *Imitations of Horace*, that a proposed extension to Bathurst's estate would result in the demolition of some buildings at Sapperton:

> Alas, my Bathurst! what will they avail?
> Join Cotswood hills to Saperton's fair dale,
> Let rising granaries and temples here,
> There mingled farms and pyramids appear,
> Link towns to towns with avenues of oak,
> Enclose whole downs in walls – 'tis all a joke!
> Inexorable Death shall level all,
> And trees, and stones, and farms, and farmer fall.

Sapperton lies just beyond the western fringe of Cirencester Park, a mile south of Park Corner, where Byng was forced to seek shelter under an old beech tree (of all things) during a severe thunderstorm, and where the 'Spiritual Quixote' and his Sancho Panza, hoping to find refreshment at a quiet inn, found instead that the hostelry to which they had been directed was overflowing with race crowds from Cirencester. Geoffry Wildgoose, moved by the Spirit to harangue the gathered company, just as he had on Dover's Hill, and unwilling to learn from his earlier experience, only succeeded in calling forth buckets of cold water on his own head and that of the hapless Jerry Tugwell.

One of Sapperton's major attractions was the tunnel, opened in 1789, which carried the Thames and Severn Canal for more than two miles under the Cotswolds, from close by The Daneway Inn (formerly The Bricklayer's Arms) at the Sapperton end, until it emerged into open daylight once again near Coates. Byng was at hand, after extricating himself from the 'gloomy' avenues of Cirencester Park, to explore the workings of the tunnel while it was still under construction, during the summer of 1787. His diary contains a graphic contemporary account of the working conditions under which this massive feat of engineering was accomplished:

> Nothing cou'd be more gloomy than thus being dragg'd into the bowels of the earth, rumbling and jumbling through mud, and over stones, with a small lighted candle in my hand . . . When the last peep of daylight vanish'd, I was enveloped in thick smoke arising from the gunpowder of the miners, at whom, after passing by many labourers who work by small candles, I did at last arrive; they come from the Derbyshire and Cornish mines, are in eternal danger and frequently perish by falls of earth . . . The return of warmth and happy daylight I hail'd with pleasure, having journey'd a mile of darkness.

One can only admire Byng's bravery and spirit of adventure in penetrating the tunnel workings in such uncertain conditions.

E. Temple Thurston, travelling in his canal boat, *The Flower of Gloster,* made a journey through Sapperton Tunnel in 1911, very shortly before it fell into disuse. 'Into the dim darkness

Western entrance to Sapperton Tunnel, 1912

you glide,' he explained, 'and, within half an hour, are lost in a lightless cavern where the drip drip of the clammy water sounds incessantly in your ears.' It took Temple Thurston and his travelling companion, Eynsham Harry, four hours to 'leg' their way through the tunnel, by propelling the barge with their feet along the side walls. 'It was evening when we came out into the light again,' he recalled, 'and though the sun had set, with shadows falling everywhere, it almost dazzled me.'

For many years Sapperton was the home of Norman Jewson who, although not primarily a writer himself but a distinguished architect, closely associated with Ernest Gimson, nevertheless produced a delightful volume of reminiscences, *By Chance I Did Rove*, which was first published in a private and limited edition in 1951, and later reprinted several times to gain a much wider audience. Jewson lived in Gloucestershire for nearly seventy years, initially at Frampton Mansell for a short time and equally briefly at Oakridge Lynch, before settling in nearby Sapperton, a village he first set eyes on in 1907, and which he came to regard, by all accounts, as an 'Arcadian place'.

Jewson was employed by Gimson at the workshop of Cotswold-influenced architects and craftsmen then based at Daneway House. Shortly after he moved to Sapperton, Jewson was joined at his cottage by Walter Gissing, who was taken on as a pupil by Gimson in 1910. Walter was the son of the Yorkshire-born novelist George Gissing – a prolific writer and the author of *New Grub Street* – who had died some years earlier, and the nephew of Algernon Gissing, 'a cheerful, bustling little man', according to Jewson. Towards the end of his life Algernon Gissing produced a piece of classic Cotswold literature in his book *The Footpath-Way in Gloucestershire*, which appeared in 1924.

Walter Gissing, it seems, inherited his famous but sadly underrated father's morose tendencies, although he made a great success of his work with Gimson, a career that was unfortunately cut short when he was killed in action during the First World War. Jewson recalled that the young man was passionately fond of music and spent many of his free evenings in Cirencester, where he played the church organ.

Before Gimson's workshops were moved to Daneway House, in around 1904, they had been established for over a decade at Pinbury Park, one-and-a-half miles north of Sapperton, a medium-sized grey Cotswold stone house dating from the seventeenth century, which became John Masefield's home in 1933. Masefield was in his mid-fifties, and had already been Poet Laureate for three years, by the time he arrived at Sapperton, a move that had been precipitated by the illness of his wife, Constance, who had undergone a successful operation for the removal of a brain tumour in 1932. Mrs Masefield was considerably weakened by the experience, however, and the adoption of a quieter lifestyle became essential.

The Masefields had been living at Boar's Hill, Oxford, where they were at the centre of many activities, not least the organization of their stylish amateur theatrical productions, but perhaps the couple would have moved anyway. In 1929 Masefield, who was a countryman to the core, had written to tell his friend, the poet Laurence Binyon, that Boar's Hill 'is no longer pleasant, but a thrusting suburb'.

Pinbury Park, once the home of Robert Atkyns, author of *The Ancient and Present State of Gloucestershire*, which was first published in 1712, seemed an ideal place for Constance to recruit her strength. The Masefields rented this secluded property from Earl Bathurst. A former house on the site had once been a nunnery, and an avenue of yews there is still known as Nuns Walk, along which, recalled Jewson, the ghost

Pinbury Park, Sapperton

of the nun-housekeeper was said to roll Double Gloucester cheeses! The present house has an attractive sunken garden, with an uninterrupted view over a wooded hillside, and still retains its air of isolation.

Sapperton no doubt appealed to Masefield on several levels. The landscape was highly reminiscent of that in which he had spent his Herefordshire childhood and, as he was particularly fascinated by waterways, he would have relished the connection with Sapperton Tunnel, even though it had fallen into disuse over twenty years before he moved to the village.

Masefield was at the height of his fame, on both sides of the Atlantic, during the years he lived at Pinbury Park and, although well past middle age, he was still in vigorous good health. It was during this period that he was awarded the prestigious Order of Merit by George V for his services to literature, and in 1937 he became president of the Society of Authors. Among his published works to appear at this time were two of his most enduring novels for children: *Dead Ned* and the much-televised *Box of Delights*.

Although the Masefields were obliged to reduce the scale of their social life for a while following Constance's illness, their new home was often filled with welcome guests. Neville Coghill and Laurence Whistler were just two of the many visitors who came over – some from Oxford, others from London or elsewhere – to join in with outdoor games such as bowls or croquet during the day, and chess or backgammon in the evening.

Despite its obvious attractions during the summer, Pinbury Park had several distinct drawbacks in the winter months. The house was notoriously difficult to heat in Masefield's day, and the pipes froze with monotonous regularity in the cold weather. The exasperation that Masefield must have felt occasionally when the snow came and the house became cut off, making it extremely difficult for a popular and busy Poet Laureate to go about his daily affairs, was reflected in a diary entry of the period: 'Deep, deep the drift – what tons to shift', he recorded, drily. As a result the Masefields spent several winters abroad in search of warmer climates, returning to Pinbury Park only with the spring.

Had Masefield ever spent a Christmas Eve at home, though, his spirits would doubtless have been much improved by a visit to The Carpenter's Arms at nearby Miserden, judging by the cosy picture drawn by Warren. There, in the hazy lamplight of the crowded bar parlour, all thoughts of deep midwinter were banished for a while, at least:

> I do not know a more attractive inn anywhere in the Cotswolds, and I have certainly never seen one so full of good-will . . . Song after song filled the smoke-blue room, everybody joining in with gusto, and quite drowning the impromptu accompaniment of the fiddler, who wandered in and out among the singing crowd, shutting his eyes and sweeping his bow up to the ceiling . . . Most of the men of the village must have been in the 'Carpenter's Arms', so large an assembly filled the smoke-dense room when we opened the door.

Given Pinbury Park's rather isolated position, and the fact that the Masefields were not getting any younger – Constance, eleven years older than her husband, was sixty-six when they moved to the house – life at Sapperton was destined, perhaps, never to be anything more than a pleasant interlude. In 1939 they returned to the scene of their early married life, when they moved to a house at Clifton Hampden – the village, incidentally, where J. Arthur Gibbs lies buried – near Abingdon, and there they spent the remainder of their years.

* * *

During his early twenties, at the turn of the twentieth century, as a bachelor living in London, Masefield had met and forged close friendships with a number of well-known figures in the literary and artistic world, some of whom he had come into contact with through the Irish poet W.B. Yeats's regular Monday soirées in Bloomsbury, and others at lectures or elsewhere. One such personality was the artist and noted portrait painter William Rothenstein who, born in 1872, was six years older than Masefield. After their first meeting, at the house of the Scottish artist, William Strang, in St John's Wood, Rothenstein described the young poet as 'a quiet youth, with eyes that seemed surprised at the sight of the world, and hair that stood up behind like a cockatoo's feathers'.

Twenty years before Masefield settled at Pinbury Park, Rothenstein went to live at nearby Iles Farm in the steep hillside hamlet of Far Oakridge. He discovered the seventeenth-century house while staying in Gloucestershire with his wife and the Indian poet Rabindranath Tagore during the summer of 1912. The artist had met Tagore during a recent visit to India, and he subsequently did much to bring the poet's work to a wider audience in Britain. Rothenstein paid £1,300 for the house, with its stone front, mullioned windows and fifty-five acres of land. 'Oh the pride with which I first explored each field, and the hanging beech wood, and the house and barn!' he wrote later. 'I was too ignorant to notice the lamentable state of the walls and fences.'

Rothenstein engaged his architect-friend Jewson to renovate the property and for seven years, from 1913, Iles Farm became the haunt of all kinds of celebrities, who arrived to be drawn or painted. The poet W.H. Davies, writing in his auto-biography, *Later Days*, recalled his own visit to Rothenstein's home at Far Oakridge:

When I reached him I found that he was spending all his mornings in painting one tree, which stood all alone in a meadow. His studio was full of this tree . . . In the afternoon, Rothenstein spent his time in working at a large oil portrait of himself. Now Rothenstein is certainly no better looking than I am . . . so when I saw [him] standing there with a large fat smile on his lips, as he painted himself by looking into a mirror – when I saw this, I felt I must either rush out of the room or strike him a heavy blow on the back of the head. However, Rothenstein's smile in the evening, when he sat with his three children, and was a father instead of an artist, was a different thing altogether.

Jewson, who spent a great deal of time at the house while the alterations were being carried out, described an evening when Tagore gave a recital of one of his long poems. 'He was an impressive, if a shade theatrical, figure in his Eastern robes as he read his poem in perfect English by moonlight on the terrace in front of the house.'

From 1914, and for the duration of the First World War, the critic, essayist and caricaturist Max Beerbohm also lived in Far Oakridge, at Winstons Cottage close to Iles Farm. Beerbohm and Rothenstein were not only neighbours but also very old friends. The two men were exactly the same age and enjoyed each other's company immensely, but, whereas Rothenstein was captivated by his tiny Gloucestershire estate overlooking the Golden Valley, to Beerbohm the countryside was anathema – a disagreeable but necessary refuge during the war years. He made only the most limited forays into his rural surroundings, and whenever he emerged from his cottage he was never less than immaculately dressed, 'as if,' recalled Jewson, 'for a garden party at Buckingham Palace'. Averse to walking any distance if he could avoid it, Beerbohm seldom ventured farther, by all accounts, than the hundred yards or so from his cottage to The Nelson Inn, where he bought his cigarettes, even then invariably taking his walking-cane and gloves. Rothenstein recalled:

During the winter he was content to stay indoors with all the windows carefully shut, and we remembered how, when

The Nelson Inn, Far Oakridge

with us, if he noticed an open window, he would stroll round the room, talking and smoking while he gradually approached the window and, as though absent-mindedly, carefully close it.

Nevertheless, Beerbohm did visit Iles Farm quite frequently, where he was a great favourite with the Rothenstein children, happily playing with them and writing amusing poems about their pets. Jewson saw him there regularly and was singularly impressed by the courtesy, charm and wit of 'the Incomparable Max'.

Beerbohm wrote several of the stories that were later collected in his volume, *Seven Men*, while living at Winstons Cottage, and he also began work there on the series of caricatures that comprised 'Rossetti and His Circle', which appeared in 1922. Jewson recalled being invited to an 'unofficial exhibition' at the cottage to view the drawings Beerbohm had made.

Hard on the heels of Beerbohm came the poet, actor and dramatist John Drinkwater, and his wife, Kathleen, who lived at Winstons Cottage for three years from 1918. Drinkwater, who was born in Leytonstone, East London, in 1882, had first been drawn to Gloucestershire by Lascelles Abercrombie and the various other poets who had congregated around Dymock, although, as he went to school in Oxford and first started work in Birmingham, he had spent a good deal of his spare time over many years exploring the Malvern Hills and the Cotswolds. In 1907 he was a co-founder of the Pilgrim Players which, six years later, blossomed into the world-renowned Birmingham Repertory Theatre, with Drinkwater as its manager. He wrote one of his most successful plays, *Abraham Lincoln*, at Winstons Cottage in 1919. One of his later plays, a comedy called *Bird in Hand*, about a squire's son who falls in love with an innkeeper's daughter, was set in a fictitious country inn, The Bird in Hand, in Gloucestershire. When it was first staged in Birmingham during the summer of 1927, in a production directed by the author, the play starred Peggy Ashcroft and Laurence Olivier, both of whom were giving early performances in their respective careers.

In his memoirs Rothenstein described the Drinkwaters as 'the best of neighbours – John the poet incarnate, generous, high-minded, enthusiastic over the work of other poets, delighting in the countryside, in his little garden, in playing host to friends in his cottage'. Drinkwater returned the compliment, by toasting Rothenstein and Iles Farm in verse:

> I celebrate
> Your hearth, your comfortable speech
> Of young years and late,
> Your courtesies that are content
> To sow and wait . . .

For his part Drinkwater thought that the area was 'the most beautiful in England . . . I am myself the tenant of a small cottage,' he wrote, 'on a byway that is passed by a stranger hardly once a week.'

Drinkwater's response to life at Far Oakridge could hardly have been more removed from Beerbohm's abhorrence of country life, a contrast that was neatly summed up by the two famous tenants of Winstons Cottage themselves, each of whom wrote a poem expressing their feelings for the place. Drinkwater's beautiful 'Cottage Song' begins:

> Morning and night I bring
> Clear water from the spring,
> And through the lyric noon
> I hear the larks in tune,
> And when the shadows fall
> There's providence for all.

Beerbohm's witty and 'wicked echo of so lovely a poem' is called 'Same Cottage – but Another Song, of Another Season':

> Morning and night I found
> White snow upon the ground,
> And on the tragic well
> Grey ice had cast her spell.
> A dearth of wood and coal
> Lay heavy on my soul.

CHAPTER EIGHT

All Up and Down Hill

From Far Oakridge the most direct route to Stroud, five miles or so to the west, lies through the Golden Valley, a steep-sided cleft divided by the River Frome and the Thames & Severn Canal. The name originated in more affluent times when the cloth-making industry ensured the area's prosperity during the eighteenth and early nineteenth centuries, and it is largely justified today by the autumn brilliance of the beech woods that line the valley's course between Sapperton and Frampton Mansell.

The population of the cloth-making valleys in the Stroud area was brought to its knees when the industry collapsed in the early years of the nineteenth century. Riding north from Tetbury, in September 1826, through Avening, Nailsworth and Woodchester, William Cobbett recorded in *Rural Rides*, the doleful scene that met his eyes:

> The work and the trade is so flat that in, I should think, much more than a hundred acres of ground, which I have seen today, covered with rails, or racks, for the drying of cloth, I do not think that I have seen one single acre where the racks had cloth upon them. The workmen do not get half wages; great numbers are thrown on the parish; but the Gloucestershire people have no notion of dying with hunger; and it is with great pleasure that I remark that I have seen no woe worn creature this day.

A hundred years earlier Daniel Defoe had encountered the industry in full swing, as he reported in his *Tour through the*

Whole Island of Great Britain:

> Gloucestershire must not be passed over without some
> account of a most pleasant and fruitful vale . . . which is
> called Stroud Water; famous not for the finest cloths only,
> but for dyeing those cloths of the finest scarlets, and other
> grain colours that are anywhere in England; perhaps in any
> part of the world.

Today Stroud is a populous town of nearly forty thousand
inhabitants; a thriving centre for business, light industry and
the arts, where valleys, roads and rivers meet. As such it is an
excellent starting point from which to explore the literary
connections of south-west Gloucestershire.

* * *

Travelling north from Stroud you arrive, after a few miles, at
Edge, where Max Beerbohm lived briefly at Highcroft before
finally returning to Italy in September 1947. Towards the end
of the Second World War Beerbohm and his wife, Florence,
had been bombed out of the cottage they were renting in
Surrey. An old friend who lived in California lent them
Highcroft and they stayed there for a year. Once again
Beerbohm is chiefly remembered by some of the older local
residents for always being immaculately dressed and for
walking no farther than the village shop (now extinct) to buy
his cigarettes.

It was while he was living in the nearby hamlet of Stockend
that C. Henry Warren wrote *A Cotswold Year*, which appeared
in 1936. Stockend, which he calls 'Woodend' in the book, was,
indeed still is, an isolated spot, very much off the beaten track,
and a place, he said, that

> still keeps very much to itself. Living in the frugal hills, its
> inhabitants enjoy a precarious hold on life; and poverty is
> still an outlaw. Their language is in the main homespun . . .

Their road, if such it can be called that has never had a penny spent on it out of the rates, is a patched-up affair . . . And their cottages are hidden under the shelter of the woods and are subject to the critical eyes of none but themselves. Those things, and the inaccessibility of the place, have always made Woodenders very much a law unto themselves.

* * *

Isolated though it is, and even more so at the end of the nineteenth century, Beatrix Potter might well have visited Stockend herself, when she was in search of local cottage interiors to sketch for one of her stories, while staying only a mile away at Harescombe Grange. She was already twenty-eight when, in June 1894, she paid her first visit to the home of her distant relations, the Huttons, near Stroud. Although she was probably unaware of it at the time, her career as a writer and illustrator of children's books had already begun when,

Harescombe Grange, near Stroud, late nineteenth century

during the previous autumn, she had written to Noel Moore, the five-year-old son of her former companion, Annie Carter, sending him a lively account – with pen-and-ink drawings – of Peter Rabbit's adventures in Mr McGregor's garden. This 'picture letter' was the forerunner of many she was to send to young correspondents over the next few years, and from which she later developed the ideas for some of her stories. The letter to Noel Moore eventually grew into *The Tale of Peter Rabbit*, which first appeared in 1901.

In the meantime, however, a visit to Harescombe Grange was a rare treat for Potter – 'like a most pleasant dream', as she described it later – and marked the first occasion in almost five years when she had travelled independently of her parents, for, despite her age, she was seldom allowed to go away from home alone. Born in 1866 into a wealthy family, she had always led a sheltered existence, as a self-sufficient child absorbed in her own interests and doomed to long, solitary days in the nursery. As a young woman she lived unobtrusively in the shadow of her parents, and in a household where the pattern of each day conformed to the same rigid timetable.

That first holiday was a foretaste of several similar visits that Potter was to make to Gloucestershire over the next few years. In the detailed journal she kept at the time, which was written in a secret code of her own invention (the code was deciphered by Leslie Linder during the 1950s, and the journal subsequently published in 1966, to coincide with the centenary of her birth), Potter accurately described Stroud, where she had arrived from London by train, as 'all up and down hill, a straggling country town, devoted to brewers and some dye works'.

Potter's distant cousin and close friend, Caroline Hutton, had travelled with her from Paddington and, after arriving at Stroud, the two young ladies had made the rest of their way to Harescombe Grange in a large open fly, a journey that proved something of a trial for the poor beast that was employed to pull them along. The house, which is still in the hands of the Hutton family today, stands on a steep hillside with enviable views of the surrounding country. Potter was enchanted by everything around her: the smell of bean fields and new-mown hay, the grey stone mills nestling in deep valleys and the steep country roads. The only cloud on her horizon was meeting the Huttons themselves, none of whom she had ever seen except for Caroline, and she was decidedly nervous at the prospect.

However, as her journal records, she was pleasantly surprised by Caroline's father, a local magistrate, whom she had been led to believe 'by universal report as an austere man'. Her own assessment was somewhat different: 'I soon came to the conclusion that he is one of the kindest of old gentlemen, and certainly a character.'

Potter had not been at Harescombe Grange for more than a few days when she discovered at first hand just how outlandish a place Stockend really was. As Warren explained in the 1930s, it had once been a hamlet of ill-repute, a place where, even in his day, so he said, ladies were 'still inclined to tread warily'. Apparently, she confided to her journal, Mr Seddon, the vicar of Painswick,

> reported [to Mr Hutton] that certain squatters had had a drinking bout on Sunday in a cottage at Stockend. It was a question whether coin had passed and whether it could be proved. Even Mr. Hutton's ingenuity was baffled.

She and Caroline spent a considerable amount of time together, exploring the grounds of Harescombe Grange and the countryside around the village. Potter was greatly intrigued, in Harescombe itself, by the thirteenth-century church of St John the Baptist, with its 'curious belfry and a handsome Saxon font', and by Sam Fluck's cottage, with its walls covered in roses and honeysuckle. 'I thought some of the young men were rather fine looking,' she noted, 'and some of the young women pretty, but they wear badly, poor wages, and I should say unhealthy in the combes.'

It was almost inevitable that, sooner or later, her repeated visits over the years to Harescombe Grange would provide Potter with the inspiration for a story and, in due course, they did so with double measure. On one occasion, while she was staying at the house, two mice were caught in a cage-trap in the kitchen and, rather than allow them to be killed, Potter rescued them and took them home to Bolton Gardens in Kensington, where they became firmly established as her pets. She called them Hunca Munca and Tom Thumb, and used them as models for the illustrations she drew in her story *The Tale of Two Bad Mice*, which was published in 1904.

One of Potter's most famous stories, however, and one certainly with more local interest, grew out of an incident that had been related to her by Caroline who, in turn, had heard the details from an elderly neighbour at Harescombe. The account of the tailor, the waistcoat and the 'No more twist' so captured her imagination that she wove a story of her own around it. *The Tailor of Gloucester* has since become one of her best-loved tales, 'And the queerest thing about it,' she wrote, 'is – that I heard it in Gloucestershire, and that it is true.'

As the years passed, Potter became increasingly absorbed in writing and illustrating and, from 1901 onwards, published twenty of her 'little books' for children – as she described them – in fewer than the same number of years. She was much preoccupied with farming in the Lake District as well. In 1905, when she was approaching forty, Potter purchased Hill Top Farm at Near Sawrey, a village of traditional Lakeland cottages, flanked by Esthwaite Water and Windermere. It was from this picturesque corner that she drew the inspiration for so many of her stories. Visits to Gloucestershire became rarer until they ceased altogether, but the two cousins remained firm friends into their old age.

When, in 1913, Potter was experiencing considerable opposition from her parents over her intention to marry William Heelis (Heelis was merely a country solicitor at Hawkshead, while the Potters belonged 'to the Bar and the Bench'), it was to her cousin at Harescombe Grange that she wrote appealing for moral support. Caroline replied immediately, advising her 'to marry him quietly in spite of them'. Potter followed her cousin's advice and, for the last thirty years of her life, enjoyed a degree of happiness and fulfilment that she had not known hitherto, as a busy working farmer and a highly respected breeder of Herdwick sheep.

* * *

From Harescombe Grange the shortest route to Slad, two miles north-east of Stroud, is by way of country lanes, 'all up and down hill' and all so narrow that there is, in places, barely sufficient room for an average-sized car to negotiate its passage between the hedgerows and dry-stone walls. It is well worth breaking this sometimes tortuous journey at Painswick, if only to saunter along the avenues of clipped yews in the town's magnificent churchyard, where the nineteenth-century poet Sydney Dobell, who spent most of his life in Gloucestershire, lies buried.

Slad, a mile south of Bulls Cross on the B4070, is, as the whole world knows, the tiny village where the Gloucestershire poet and author Laurie Lee spent his childhood and that he has immortalized for countless readers in *Cider With Rosie*, the first volume of his autobiographical trilogy. Lee recalled:

> I was set down from the carrier's cart at the age of three and there with a sense of bewilderment and terror my life in the village began . . . I don't know where I lived before then. My life began on the carrier's cart which brought me up the long slow hills to the village, and dumped me in the high grass, and lost me.

Lee's mother, Annie, was born at Quedgeley during the 1880s. She was the daughter of a Berkeley coachman, who later turned publican and became the landlord of The Plough at Sheepscombe. Annie helped her father to run the pub for a while after her mother's death but, later, she took a job as a housekeeper to a widower with four children. Before long she had fallen in love with and married her employer, but the marriage came to an end when Mr Lee joined the army in 1917. Shortly afterwards, Annie Lee arrived in Slad with a brood of eight children to look after: four of her own, and the four she had inherited from the husband who had recently deserted her.

The Slad of Lee's 1920s boyhood is more-or-less recognizable today, yet at the same time it has altered drastically. Most of the familiar landmarks that he wrote about are still there: Frith Wood (named Brith Wood by Lee); the war memorial, scene of an unsolved murder; Steanbridge House, once the home of Squire Jones; The Woolpack, which now boasts a 'Cider With Rosie' bar, and, most important of all, perhaps, the steep-sided Slad Valley itself, 'a jungly, bird-crammed, insect-hopping sun-trap whenever there happened to be any sun', which nothing except a major calamity could ever seriously alter. More to the point, the seventeenth-century house built of Cotswold stone and now called Rosebank, where Lee spent his famous childhood, can still be seen crouching in a deep well at the head of a lane that turns off sharply from the Stroud road, just above The Woolpack. Even today, looking down on this T-shaped affair of a house that, in an earlier incarnation, had been a pub, it is easy to imagine young Lee and his family living cheek by jowl with snuff-taking Granny Trill and wine-making Granny Wallon. These were the 'Grannies in the Wainscot', always at daggers drawn yet thriving on their enmity, who, although each had their separate accommodation, shared the building with the Lees.

Rosebank, Slad, where Laurie Lee spent his childhood

Yet, as W.B. Yeats said, although in a slightly different context, all is changed, changed utterly and, as an adolescent, Lee himself witnessed the beginnings of the metamorphosis of his own village:

The last days of my childhood were also the last days of the village. I belonged to that generation which saw, by chance, an end of a thousand years' life . . . Soon the village would break, dissolve and scatter, become no more than a place for pensioners. It had a few years left, the last of its thousand, and they passed almost without our knowing. They passed quickly, painlessly, in motor-bike jaunts, in the shadows of the new picture-palace, in quick trips to Gloucester (once a foreign city) to gaze at the jazzy shops. Yet right to the end, like the false strength that precedes death, the old life seemed as lusty as ever.

A similar story was being duplicated at about the same time throughout the land, as Fred Archer confirmed farther north at Ashton-under-Hill:

> In the early 1920s, there were about three cars in our village. Little did I think that fifty years later I'd be looking both ways twice before crossing the road. In those days I saw a busy road not of motor traffic but people, animals, to and fro from morning until night.

Even so the young Lee would no doubt have found it impossible to predict, when he saw that first brass-lamped motor car come coughing up the hill from the direction of Stroud in the late 1920s, the speed and frequency with which traffic of all description would hurtle downhill through the village above his old home, causing a slight rush of cold air to pass through the open door of The Woolpack, and destroying

The Woolpack Inn, Slad, c. 1920

the once peaceful isolation of Slad for ever. This change would have been an unmitigated disaster were it not for *Cider With Rosie*, a work of prose constructed by a consummate poet and filled with vivid recollections and images of a fast-vanishing age, so that to read it is almost like visiting a foreign country.

A veil was drawn across this epoch in Slad's history when, at the age of nineteen, Lee left the village and, as he explained, closed that part of his life for ever. Aware that a small, enclosed community can be at the same time a cocoon and a prison, he was driven away – like thousands before him – by that powerful urge, particularly strong in youth, to discover what lay beyond the horizon. *As I Walked Out One Midsummer Morning*, the sequel to *Cider With Rosie*, recalls the moment of departure: 'The stooping figure of my mother, waist-deep in the grass and caught there like a piece of sheep's wool,' he wrote, 'was the last I saw of my country home as I left it to discover the world.' Lee was to return from time to time, and he came back to live in the village again in old age, but no one would seriously pretend that Slad could ever be quite as it was before the twentieth century had belatedly knocked on its door and so boldly swept in.

CHAPTER NINE

A Scholar and a Tramp

The twin villages that comprise the parish of Woodchester are spread out over a steep hillside towering above the Bath road, two miles south of Stroud. North and South Woodchester are linked by a network of precipitous, narrow lanes bordered by grey stone houses, with a cosmopolitan range of light industry occupying the mills, which were once exclusively devoted to wool, scattered in the valley below.

Turning off the road to South Woodchester, through a narrow opening flanked by two stone pillars, a long drive, curving through neat farmland, eventually arrives at Woodchester House. This solid eighteenth-century, grey stone building, which rests on a sharp incline, is, to all outward appearances, little changed from the days when the poet, Alfred Edward Housman, was a regular visitor there. Housman's parents were married in Woodchester, in June 1858, but shortly afterwards they went to live at Fockbury, near Bromsgrove, where Housman's father, Edward, had been brought up. Housman was born there, at the Valley House, in 1859.

Housman paid his first visit to Woodchester while he was still only a young boy, during the 1860s, taken there by his mother, Sarah Jane, who was the daughter of a former rector of the village. He never met his grandfather, who died shortly before Edward and Sarah Jane's wedding, but he would have found much to admire in the Reverend John Williams, who was a classical scholar with a distinct talent for writing verse. Sarah Jane inherited her father's poetic ability to a certain extent, but it was a gift that would find its fullest expression in her own son, some years later.

Woodchester House had once been occupied by some cousins of Edward Housman's, and it was their presence, no doubt, that had originally drawn him to the village. But when they moved away, the house was taken over by Mr and Mrs Wise, with whom Edward and his wife were also very friendly. Mr Wise was the owner of a local cloth mill and his wife, who was a particular friend of Sarah Jane's, became Alfred Housman's godmother. The Wises had three children of their own – Edith, Minnie and Edward – all of whom were somewhat older than Alfred. But when Sarah Jane died at home on her son's twelfth birthday, while he had been sent away to stay at Woodchester House during her final illness, the poignancy of the young boy's situation was not lost on Mrs Wise who, no doubt with her own three children in mind, reflected on the fact that she was exactly the same age as the

Woodchester House, A.E. Housman's 'second' home

boy's mother. Henceforth the Wises became Alfred Housman's surrogate family, and for much of his life Woodchester House was to be his second home.

Edith, Minnie and Edward Wise became Housman's closest friends, so that he was drawn back to Gloucestershire to visit them for at least a couple of days, and frequently for longer periods, almost annually, right into old age. By the end of the First World War, and with their parents long deceased, the three children, still living together in the old family home, were less prosperous than they had once been and were elderly themselves. But they had managed to cling on to Woodchester House by the simple expedient of taking in paying guests. Eventually, however, they were forced to sell up and take a much smaller property in North Woodchester.

Clearly Housman came to regard himself almost as a local inhabitant. Writing to his sister, Kate, on one occasion, he described a family who had recently moved into the village as 'quite newcomers', and he found himself much in demand when the fine Roman pavement in the churchyard was reopened for viewing during the summer of 1926. 'I was dragged in to make speeches explaining it,' he told Kate, 'as there were few local orators to do so, and the visitors were very ignorant and very grateful.' The pavement, nearly fifty feet square and apparently one of the finest Roman mosaics to have been discovered north of the Alps, originally came to light during excavations conducted by Samuel Lysons in the 1790s, on the site of what is thought to be one of Britain's biggest Roman villas.

By the mid-1920s Housman had become not only a famous poet but also a Cambridge professor. After leaving Oxford without a degree he had worked as an assistant teacher in Bromsgrove, and as a clerk at the Patent Office, before he was appointed Professor of Latin at University College, London, in 1892. He gained the post largely on the strength of the reputation he had built up as a classical scholar, through private study at the British Museum and by the publication of a series of learned papers on Greek and Latin subjects. It was while at University College that he wrote *A Shropshire Lad*, a sequence of sixty-three poems that were first printed at his own expense in 1896, and which eventually, together with his *Last Poems*, published in 1922, secured his position as one of the twentieth century's great poets.

Housman possessed a not entirely unmerited reputation for being austere and slightly aloof. 'I am not a social butterfly . . . nature meant me for solitude and meditation,' he wrote, only half-jokingly, when refusing a dinner invitation on one occasion. His biographer, Richard Perceval Graves, writing in *The Scholar-Poet* (1979), gives some idea of the impression made by the author of *A Shropshire Lad* on his students. 'Reserved', 'unapproachable', 'austere' and 'aloof' are certainly some of the adjectives applied to him, but, 'in spite of this, we all liked him in a kind of way,' wrote the archaeologist, Mortimer Wheeler, 'and felt a certain awe of him as a man of mystery and manifest ability'. It was a different story at Woodchester, however, where, for a brief period each summer, Housman was able to enjoy the company of the small number of people with whom he truly felt at home.

* * *

Just over a mile to the south-east of Woodchester lies Amberley, perched on the western edge of Minchinhampton Common. A neat and self-contained village, its position high up on the scarp invests it with a genuine sense of isolation. Sydney Dobell and his invalid wife arrived there during the summer of 1853 to spend a few quiet weeks lodging in a hillside cottage. They had been living at Coxhorne, a Georgian house in the village of Charlton Kings (now a suburb of Cheltenham), but they were shortly to leave for Edinburgh where they were due to consult specialists about Mrs Dobell's condition. In the meantime her doctors hoped that she might derive some temporary benefit, at least, from the bracing air of this wide expanse of common.

Dobell, who although only approaching thirty was himself already suffering the initial symptoms of an illness that was to plague him for the remainder of his life, completed his long dramatic poem, 'Balder', during this peaceful interlude at Amberley. Published in 1854, it relates the tragic story of a poet who kills his wife when she becomes mad after the death of their baby. This somewhat grim tale, dubbed a product of the 'Spasmodic School' – a small group of now entirely overlooked poets, including Dobell himself, who specialized in intense psychological dramas – was a successor to 'The Roman', which had appeared in 1850.

Mrs Craik was drawn to the exposed and windy heights of Amberley during the mid-1850s, while she was in the throes of writing *John Halifax, Gentleman*. She lodged at Rose Cottage and, before long, had set about weaving the house, the village and its surroundings into her Tewkesbury-based novel. Amberley became 'Enderley' in her tale, a retired spot where John Halifax took his friend Phineas Fletcher to recuperate after an illness. 'Such a nice, nice place, on the slope of Enderley Hill . . . A cottage – Rose Cottage – for it's all in a bush of cluster-roses, up to the very roof . . . Shouldn't you like to live on a hill-side, to be at the top of everything?' John enquires of the tanner's son. 'Well, that's Enderley . . . But oh, the blessed quiet and solitude of the place.'

It was at Rose Cottage that John Halifax first met his future wife, Ursula March, if one discounts that other occasion many years earlier when, as a little girl staying at the mayor's house, she had offered bread to the hungry young beggar-lad on the streets of Norton Bury. Ursula and her ailing father were the temporary tenants of the other half of Rose Cottage when John and Phineas were lodging there.

Towards the end of their lives John and Ursula actually moved to Enderley, where they lived with their children at Beechwood Hall, a house for which Craik is said to have used Amberley Court as her model. 'It was,' she explained, 'the

Rose Cottage, Amberley, 'all in a bush of cluster-roses, up to the very roof . . .'

"great house" at Enderley, just on the slope of the hill below Rose Cottage,' and she set much of the action in the later part of her novel around this rambling, nineteenth-century building.

* * *

From Amberley a series of old packhorse routes winds steeply down from Minchinhampton Common to Nailsworth, a town that thrived with the prosperity of the Golden Valley and where the old woollen mills have once again been put to modern industrial uses. W.H. Davies, the so-called 'tramp-poet', chose to end his days there, living in no less than four different houses during the nine years leading up to his death in 1940.

After leaving school, Newport-born Davies served an apprenticeship to a picture-frame maker in Bristol. He soon turned his back on a conventional life and, at the age of twenty-two, sailed to America where, for many years, he lived as a hobo. He travelled restlessly from one state to another, occasionally finding himself in jail after inadvertently committing minor breaches of local state law. But his life on the road was brought to an abrupt and premature end when he lost his right leg in a railway accident while 'jumping' a freight train in Canada.

Davies returned to England where there was a small legacy of ten shillings a week, left to him by his grandmother, accruing in his absence. He lodged at various doss-houses in London and began to write poetry, initially arranging for his work to be printed privately and at his own expense. The turning point in his literary fortunes came in late 1904 when he was 'discovered' by Edward Thomas, who wrote a favourable review of Davies's slim volume of poetry, *The Soul's Destroyer*, in the *Daily Chronicle*. The two men became close friends, and it was with Thomas's encouragement that Davies wrote his *Autobiography of a Super-Tramp* (1908), for which – together with its sequel, *Later Days*, published in 1925 – he is probably best remembered by modern readers.

In keeping with his natural inclination to flout convention, Davies, although he had genuinely lived as a hobo, never conformed to the popular image of a vagrant. He was a true 'gentleman of the road', as Helen Thomas explained in her memoir of him:

> Davies had none of the attributes which one might associate with a tramp. He was not tough or callous or rough, and his manners were gentle and sensitive, especially to children and animals, and in his dress and personal cleanliness he was fastidious . . . To our children he was always 'Sweet William', and he remained our dear and delightful friend until Edward left for France.

It was after leading a rather bohemian life in London and various parts of Kent, and having recently settled into a late but very happy marriage with Helen Matilda Payne, a young woman barely half his age, that Davies eventually arrived in south-west Gloucestershire. However, he was by no means a stranger to the county. Not only had he stayed at Iles Farm as William Rothenstein's guest, when the artist painted Davies's portrait – 'I always feel sorry,' Davies wrote later, 'that Rothenstein had never made me a little present of his work, for sitting to him, as every other artist has done.' – but he had also visited Dymock where, judging from a couple of letters from Robert Frost to his friend Sidney Cox, it seems that Davies ruffled a few feathers among the colony of resident poets. Frost wrote from Little Iddens in May 1914:

> No one doubts that [Davies] is a very considerable poet, in spite of several faults and flaws everywhere. But his conceit is enough to make you misjudge him – Simply assinine. We have had a good deal of him at the house for the last week.

Again, writing a few months later from The Gallows, Frost told Cox how Wilfred Gibson and his wife had 'limped' Davies the two miles from The Old Nail Shop to visit the Abercrombies at Ryton, in pouring rain. 'They hurried poor Davies till the sweat broke out all over him,' explained Frost. 'It was partly out of spite. They had been having a bad time together as rivals in poetry.'

At the age of sixty Davies had chosen to make his home in Nailsworth because he loved the Cotswolds and it was close to his native Wales, and he lived there with the simplicity that had become his trademark. The only distinguishing feature of his rooms, which were otherwise rather sparsely furnished, was the collection of portraits that had been painted of him over the years, including one by Augustus John. There was also a bust by Epstein. These went with him and were proudly displayed, wherever he lived.

At Nailsworth, Davies and his wife lived at first in a detached, nineteenth-century stone-built house, called Axpills.

Afterwards they moved to The Croft, before settling, a few years later, into Yewdales, at the bottom of Spring Hill opposite the old market. It was while he was living in these various houses, which were all so close to each other, that Davies published two volumes of anecdotal essays with poems – *My Birds* and *My Garden* – both of which reflect the serenity that characterized his last years close to the Severn, a river that, from its opposite shores, had been a landmark of his childhood. In 1933 he wrote:

> Today I have played truant from my garden and gone two or three miles away to see the River Severn lying in a green valley . . . The sight of this river, the Severn, as seen from a hill in Monmouthshire, in my young days, is still fresh in my memory, and not likely to be forgotten. And that is why I make this pilgrimage today, and will do it again, and still again.

> This is the morning bright and clear,
> To stand on top of Christchurch Hill;
> We'll see the Severn looking down,
> In all his silver beauty, Love –
> Where he lies basking in the sun.

In 1938, despite having recently suffered a stroke, Davies left Yewdales and moved to Glendower, a low, two-storey cottage set high up on Watledge, off the steep, winding road to Minchinhampton Common, and with a bird's-eye view over the town. The after-effects of his illness and the strain of his artificial limb combined to make the walk up and down the long, steep hill to and from Nailsworth impossible. As a result his short, stocky figure became a rare sight on the streets of the town where, thumping along on his heavy wooden leg, some people thought he resembled a retired sea captain rather than a nature poet.

Glendower, Nailsworth

Although he was by no means a recluse, Davies was a shy man who, as Helen Thomas wrote, 'had an intense dislike of anybody's knowing about his domestic arrangements. He hated the idea of drawing attention to himself and raising questions in the minds of his neighbours.' This trait stayed with him throughout his life and, partly for that reason, he mixed very little socially at Nailsworth. The last thing he wanted was to be regarded as a local celebrity, although, by that time, his writing had reached a wide audience and he was a familiar voice on the radio, reciting his poems in a soft Welsh accent. Those who did visit him at home, however – a few old friends from his London days and, occasionally, fellow writers – found him unfailingly charming and hospitable.

Sadly Davies's tenure of Glendower was destined to be brief – he lived there for barely two-and-a-half years. Watledge was an idyllic spot and, as one of his poems suggests, he loved the 'flowery, green, bird-singing land':

> The moon that peeped as she came up
> Is clear on top with all her light.
> She rests her chin on Nailsworth Hill,
> And where she looks, the world is bright.

Even today, despite the constant drone of traffic from the busy main road far below, it is possible to savour something of the peaceful atmosphere that drew Davies to the place. Glendower is still there, its front door opening almost straight on to the narrow lane, and the cottage itself half hidden behind a riot of foliage, which, in summer, obscures a wall plaque containing his two most famous lines of verse:

> What is this life if full of care
> We have no time to stand and stare . . .

Davies compiled several anthologies and collections of his

work during his nine years at Nailsworth, the last of which, *The Loneliest Mountain and Other Poems*, he prepared at Glendower and published in 1939. There was an unequivocal air of finality in the prefatory remarks that Davies appended to this volume: 'My doctor advises that the only hope of prolonging my life is to become lazy and selfish. But, whatever happens, the present book ends my career as a living author.'

By Christmas of that same year Davies knew that his health was failing and that death was probably not far away, but he approached the end with the same degree of stoicism that had characterized his life. 'This will be my last Christmas,' he told his friend Brian Waters, and so it was. Later Waters recalled his final visit to see Davies at Glendower, which took place on an afternoon in September 1940. 'His mind was as bright as ever,' Waters explained, 'but there was a look of resignation on his face that I had not seen there before. A few days later he had another seizure and in a week he was dead.'

Davies died well content with what he had achieved on his long journey from the doss-house to his rightful place among the ranks of distinguished twentieth-century poets. 'He was,' wrote John Haines, 'a simple man, who liked simple things and wrote of the things he saw in nature with apparent simplicity, but really with great imagination.'

CHAPTER TEN

'Stinkers' Revisited

To the south of Nailsworth the main road climbs east of
Horsley, threading its way past Barton End House which, from
August 1871, served as Sydney Dobell's home for the last three
years of his life. Delicate health had brought his literary career
to a premature end long before that, but this final home, a
place 'to live and die in', as he called it, delighted him. He
suffered from a bronchial condition, and the clean air helped
him to breathe more easily. Encouraging a young friend, and
fellow poet, to visit him there, Dobell poured out his feelings
for the house in a passionate letter:

> Up here at Barton End we defy east and north winds; but the
> fact that, at the height of five hundred feet above valley-
> mists, we secure a climate more temperate than many a
> famous Italian sanatorium, is a conclusion from which I will
> earnestly beg you, in more senses than one, to arrive at the
> premises viz. Barton End House. Healthful to everyone, it
> should have a special healing for you, since, as you'll easily
> perceive, Barton is evidently either Bardon – the Bard's Hill,
> or Baldon – the hill of Apollo . . .

No doubt there were many occasions when Dobell glanced
over towards Nibley Knoll, half a dozen miles or so to the
west, a hill surmounted by a 111 ft high column erected in
1866. It is inscribed to the memory of William Tyndale, whose
rendering of the New Testament, the Pentateuch and the Book
of Jonah from the original Greek into English – a work

denounced by bishops and many copies of which were destroyed – resulted in a charge of heresy, followed by Tyndale's death at the stake in 1536. This conspicuous and recently restored monument of grey stone, which, at first glance from a distance, could easily be mistaken for one of the

Tyndale Monument, Nibley Knoll, North Nibley

woollen mill chimneys so common in this part of Gloucestershire, lies in the path of the Cotswold Way. On a clear day the
view from the tower's summit, embracing the Cotswolds,
Malverns and Brecons, is breathtaking, and available to
anyone who is prepared to collect the key from a nearby house
and climb the column's 123 steps. But the memorial itself is
superfluous, erected, it would seem, in error.

For many years it was confidently believed that Tyndale had
been born at Hunt's Court, an ancient farmhouse in the village
of North Nibley, which rests in the Knoll's shadow. Certainly
the Victorians thought so, for it was they who built the tower
in his memory, but there are several other contenders for his
birthplace: for example Hurst Manor, in the parish of
Slimbridge, three or four miles away, where an oak screen in
the village church of St John's is dedicated to the sixteenth-
century scholar. Melksham Court in Stinchcombe is another
possibility. Members of the Tyndale family occupied both
Hurst Manor and Melksham Court around the time that
William Tyndale would have been growing up, but, even so, no
documentary evidence has so far come to light to establish
beyond any reasonable doubt the claim of one house over
another. However, although it is well established that Tyndale
had some connections with Gloucestershire – in 1522, for
example, he was employed as a tutor to the sons of Sir John
Walsh at Little Sodbury, a village included in the county at that
time – it now seems that the man who, to quote his own
words, sought 'to render the New Testament from the original
Greek into proper English,' in order that 'the lowly husband-
man may sing his verses at the plough and the weaver may
warble them at the shuttle', was actually born somewhere in
the Welsh Marches.

Similarly a local tradition has grown up over the centuries
that William Shakespeare lived for some time in or near
Dursley, at that early point in his life between leaving school at
Stratford-on-Avon and appearing as an actor and playwright in

London. One suggestion, that he left home and 'went to ground' after being implicated in a serious poaching incident, is impossible to prove. The seventeenth-century Wiltshire antiquary John Aubrey asserted that Shakespeare 'had been in his younger yeares as Schoolmaster in the Countrey'. But his precise whereabouts during these so-called 'lost years', usually said to extend roughly between 1585 and 1592, have been, and still are, the source of endless speculation by Shakespearian scholars. One recent and well-publicized theory placed him firmly in Lancashire at the relevant time, so the matter is clearly awash with uncertainty.

The Dursley connection has no doubt gained credence partly because Shakespeare was a well-known name in the town during the seventeenth century. R.P. Beckinsale, for example, writing in his *Companion into Gloucestershire* (1939), mentions the marriage of a Dursley weaver called Thomas Shakespeare in 1678. More to the point, perhaps, a scene in *Richard II* is set not only in Gloucestershire, but apparently in the hills above Dursley, as it contains an oblique reference to Berkeley Castle – 'the castle by yon tuft of trees' – four miles away, thereby giving much useful ammunition to those people who feel that Shakespeare must have had an intimate knowledge of the area.

'How far is it, my lord, to Berkeley now?' enquires Bolingbroke, who later became Henry IV.

'Believe me, noble lord, I am a stranger here in Gloucestershire,' replies the Earl of Northumberland. 'These high wild hills and rough uneven ways draws out our miles, and makes them wearisome.'

Furthermore, some inference has been drawn from Shakespeare's reference in *Henry IV Part 2* to 'William Visor of Woncot' and 'Clement Perkes of the hill' that he must have been familiar both with the local corruption for neighbouring

Woodmancote and the regional terminology for the wolds thereabouts.

Acquainted though he no doubt was with parts of north Gloucestershire, Shakespeare's connection with Dursley has yet to be firmly established. That he had a reasonably accurate topographical knowledge of the area, either through documentary research or personal experience, is not in question, but this does not serve as proof that he ever actually lived in the south-west corner of the county.

* * *

No such doubts surround the novelist Evelyn Waugh's connection with Stinchcombe, a village that in recent years has become almost a suburb of Dursley, lying just to the west of the town and sandwiched between the M5 on one hand and Stinchcombe Hill on the other. The latter, incidentally, boasts a golf course that is said to have the finest panoramic views of any in the country, with its distant prospect of the Welsh hills. Waugh was in his mid-thirties when he moved to Piers Court in 1937. A handsome Grade II listed building of mainly eighteenth-century origin, it was to remain his home for almost twenty years. It was during this period that many of his most famous and successful novels were written and published, including *Brideshead Revisited* (1945), *The Loved One* (1948), and the first two parts of his *Sword of Honour* trilogy: *Men at Arms* (1952) and *Officers and Gentlemen* (1955).

Waugh, the son of a publisher, was born in 1903. He was educated at Lancing and at Hertford College, Oxford, where, during his undergraduate days – among a generation of students that included Anthony Powell, Graham Greene and John Betjeman – a riotous social life took precedence over reading modern history, and resulted in a rather poor third class degree. Like a number of his contemporaries who were unable to find more congenial employment, he drifted into schoolteaching for a while, initially in far-flung Denbighshire, and then at Aston Clinton, the latter more conveniently placed, from Waugh's point of view, between Oxford and London. Although schoolmastering was not really in Waugh's line, the experience did provide him with useful 'copy' for his first novel, *Decline and Fall*, which enjoyed considerable success when it was published in 1928.

An early and unsuccessful marriage, which he embarked on around this time, was followed by an extremely restless period in Waugh's life. He made several trips abroad, which were not entirely unclouded experiences for him but, nevertheless, provided material for a number of travel books, including *Remote People* (1931), an account of his journey through Africa.

Meanwhile, at home in London, he threw himself into party-going and a hectic social whirl that would have deprived a lesser mortal of much opportunity for sustained writing. Despite these distractions, however, his career positively flourished in the wake of *Decline and Fall*, as *Vile Bodies* (1930), *Black Mischief* (1932) and *A Handful of Dust* (1934) all contributed to his growing reputation as a comic novelist of some genius. It was during the summer of 1933, while he was putting the finishing touches to *A Handful of Dust*, that Waugh met Laura Herbert, the young lady who, four years later, was to become his wife.

According to his friend and biographer, Christopher Sykes, Waugh was not really a countryman at heart. It was a combination of his marriage and the need to find a new home, together with the fact that both partners had family connections with the West Country, that drew him into that part of Gloucestershire. But he quickly settled into a pattern of life at 'Stinkers' (Waugh's nickname for Stinchcombe and Piers Court), working on his novel, *Scoop,* and redesigning the garden in Piers Court's extensive grounds, where he instituted at least two unusual features. The first, recalled his neighbour and close friend Frances Donaldson, was a path made by inverting and planting empty champagne bottles. The second was a semicircular stone wall, topped with battlements and christened 'The Edifice'. After building this astonishing folly, Waugh advertised for human skulls with which to decorate it and, according to Lady Donaldson, received a surprising number of replies!

Some of these projects, it must be admitted, were nothing more than cleverly conceived devices to stave off the ever-present threat of boredom, a condition to which Waugh was peculiarly susceptible. Lady Donaldson explained that, in addition to concocting elaborate schemes for his garden, the novelist manfully fought against this ennui in a variety of ways: 'He went for long walks over very long distances,' she recalled. 'Twice a week he spent the afternoon in the cinema in Dursley, irrespective, I think, of the film that was showing, once for each change of programme.'

While its owner was away from home on active service during the Second World War, Piers Court was occupied by a group of Dominican nuns, who ran a school there, and when Waugh and his wife eventually returned to Stinchcombe in September 1945, it was, he wrote, 'on a grey, fly-infested evening with a hangover and the excitement of homecoming contending'. Like everywhere else in Britain at the time, Piers Court was in the grip of immediate post-war austerity. He noted in his diary on 2 October:

> We have practically no meat . . . and live on eggs and macaroni, cheese (made by Laura), bread and wine; very occasionally we get a rather nasty fish. But we have some wine left. When that is gone our plight will be grave.

Writing to his friend, Randolph Churchill, a few days later, Waugh expanded on the same theme: 'Laura broods despondently over the kitchen range and periodically raises columns of black smoke, announces that our meat ration has been incinerated, and drives me to dinner at the neighbouring inn.'

Although he was elected chairman of his parish council in 1946, Waugh tended not to become too closely involved in local affairs, and, it would seem, with a fair degree of success. In 1953, for example, he told his old friend Nancy Mitford that, although he had been president of the Dursley Dramatic Society for fifteen years, he had never met one of its members! That may have been a slight exaggeration, added, perhaps, for its comic effect, but Waugh did cultivate the impression of living with a certain degree of detachment from his country neighbours at Stinchcombe and, with the notable exception of the Donaldsons, he made few friends in the local community. Indeed, a notice posted at the entrance to his drive, stating 'No Admittance on Business', was interpreted as a general discouragement to visitors.

Having remarked to his wife that he seemed to be setting himself up 'as a squire' when he first discovered Piers Court, Waugh clearly did not view himself in that light a quarter of a century later. 'A squirearchic life means sitting on the bench of magistrates and going round cattle shows,' he remarked on one

Piers Court, Stinchcombe

occasion, adding that, for him, the country was a place where he could 'be silent'.

Even a cursory examination of Waugh's published letters and diaries, however, leads one to suspect that his life was not always lived in the state of splendid isolation to which he apparently aspired. And when he did venture out into village society, it was to view his position as a local celebrity with a certain amount of wry humour. Writing, again to Mitford, in April 1946 about a recent cocktail party he had attended, presumably in Stinchcombe, 'where the smart hunting set were segregated from the dowdy village worthies in two rooms', he reported drily that 'Laura and I were put in the dowdy room, in spite of the fantasies in her hair.'

Almost from the moment he moved to Piers Court, Waugh had been afraid that Dursley would keep on expanding and that one day he would wake to find the town creeping up to his very gates. Writing to his wife from Freetown in September 1940 he told her that, were he not to return from the war, she should hold on to Piers Court for their son but, 'supposing Dursley grows and other factories spring up along the Severn and the place becomes an industrial district sell out by all means'. His fears gained momentum after the war when it did indeed seem likely that the village would be engulfed by a new town-planning scheme. As a result he was always thinking of selling the house and moving elsewhere. After considering various alternatives over the years, including, at one stage, a move to Ireland, Piers Court was eventually sold in 1956. 'This is the last day in the old home,' he wrote on 23 October. 'I am entirely delighted, elated, exhilarated.' The family moved to Combe Florey in Somerset, where Waugh died ten years later.

CHAPTER ELEVEN

. . . And Back Again!

Just across the Severn from Stinchcombe lies the Forest of Dean, that expanse of ancient and royal woodland that is generally regarded as the most secluded and self-contained corner in the whole of Gloucestershire. For the true Forester there is simply nowhere else in the world to compare with it. Local author Humphrey Phelps explains:

> He is content to remain in the Forest, is loth to live elsewhere, and if circumstances compel is consumed with an overwhelming desire to return. To the exiled Forester the noblest sight is the road which leads to the Forest.

But at least one erstwhile visitor was dismayed by what he might find lurking within its confines, for in *The Spiritual Quixote* the very name of the Forest filled Jerry Tugwell's imagination 'with ideas of wild beasts, robbers and outlaws'. But, after Geoffry Wildgoose had been able to reassure his companion that such horrors no longer existed,

> they jogged on pretty peaceably all the fore part of the day; and about dinner-time, coming to a fine tuft of oaks, on a bank by the side of a crystal brook, the coolness of the scene invited them to rest a little in the heat of the day, and to regale themselves with the contents of Jerry's wallet [which had been] liberally furnished with provisions the previous day.

As one of the country's largest ancient woodlands, the Forest was once an invaluable source of timber for the ships of the British Navy. It was in his capacity as Clerk of the Acts at the Navy Office that the diarist Samuel Pepys visited the Forest of Dean during the summer of 1671 – just a year before his appointment as Secretary to the Admiralty – to inspect the timber urgently needed by a British fleet that was preparing for war with Holland.

Pepys, who was born the son of a London tailor in 1633, witnessed some of the most chaotic times in England's history, from the outbreak of civil war, followed by the execution of Charles I in 1640, through to the so-called 'glorious revolution' of 1688. The period covered by his diary, which he opened on 1 January 1660 and maintained for almost ten years, included the Restoration, the Plague and the Great Fire of London. As such Pepys left behind not only an intimate and often amusing record of his daily activities and frequent indiscretions, but also first-hand accounts of these momentous events, thereby furnishing historians with an invaluable primary source, ever since the diary was first published in 1825.

Pepys closed his diary for the last time on 31 May 1669 in the mistaken belief that he was going blind: 'And this ends all that I shall ever be able to do with my own eyes in the keeping of my journal,' he recorded. As a result we have been denied a first-hand, and what would undoubtedly have been a highly idiosyncratic account of his adventures at Mitcheldean, from where he and his men undertook their survey of the Forest.

Instead we have to rely on the report that Pepys subsequently presented to Charles II, in which he clearly found that matters were far from satisfactory. Out of the ten thousand trees inspected, about half of which were oaks, he concluded that no more than eight hundred were fit for naval service. Furthermore a great many suitable trees had already been felled, but had lain so long that 'few were worth transporting,' he recorded, 'and all were likely to be useless if they lay much longer'.

Exactly 110 years later, in June 1781, John Byng arrived at Mitcheldean during his extensive 'Tour to the West' – a meandering journey that took him over six hundred miles that summer – reaching the Forest after following a route that took him through Gloucester, Huntley and Longhope 'by most pleasing lanes surrounded by orchards'. He had made a special detour to visit the Forest of Dean which, he explained,

> I was very anxious to see (as a place of fame), and was one principal object of my ride. It fully answer'd my hopes, being as enchanting as a profusion of noble trees, hawthorns, hollies on bold scenery can make it.

Byng took a leisurely ride through the Forest from Mitcheldean to a mile or so above Coleford, experiencing at first hand the 'awful grandeur' of the place, a sensation that was heightened for him by a gloomy and still evening, with the sky overhead partially obscured by the

> noble waving woods, hill above hill. The people about this country are stout and tall as I fancy all men are in warm rich soils, and where fuel is plenty. Those men who are not black'd by coals and furnaces are redded by the iron ore.

Two days later, and with a complete change in the weather, Byng was plodding northwards along the western shores of the Severn, with the Forest of Dean towering over him to the left, the wind and rain lashing his face, and a wide, open prospect of the river before him. Following his usual practice, 'to stop (if possible) about noon, at a second-rate inn, and take the family fare', something that had the considerable advantage, so Byng discovered, of costing less than half the price of an ordered dinner, he entered The Bear Inn at Newnham, 'with a good appetite, and found a round of beef just taken from the pot, which,' he boasted manfully, 'I strove to devour, and likewise a gooseberry pie'.

By a strange coincidence Pepys and his small party had stopped to dine at Newnham, too. A bill for their meal has been preserved and shows that Byng was by no means the first illustrious traveller to enjoy a good repast at a fair price in this delightful Severn-side town: a leg of mutton and cauliflower, a breast of veal, six chickens, artichokes, peas, oranges and other fruit, and cheese, all for under £1.50, with enough wine for the party adding less than 20p to the total!

John Moore, who is usually associated with Tewkesbury and north Gloucestershire, also wrote about the Forest of Dean with great affection and understanding in one of his shorter and less well-known novels, *The White Sparrow*, which was published in 1954. For his young character, Tommy Debrett, the Forest was simply 'so vast, so dark, so mysterious a place, that [he] felt sure its inmost depths must be inhabited by heraldic beasts, by the unicorns and green dragons he had seen upon inn signs'.

In more recent years, of course, Winifred Foley has become one of the Forest's most celebrated literary figures. Her several volumes of autobiography, beginning with *A Child in the Forest*, which appeared in 1974 when she was sixty, have provided a humorous and often moving insight into her own experience of life there, during the years immediately following the First World War. Her upbringing was dogged by poverty but enriched by a sense of community. 'We were content to be a race apart,' she explained, 'made up mostly of families who had lived in the Forest for generations, sharing the same handful of surnames, and speaking a dialect quite distinct from any other.'

Traditionally the Forest of Dean has been a place of charcoal burners and Free Miners, the latter of whom, wrote Moore, 'served no bosses, obeyed no hooters, worked for as long or as briefly as they chose and received no weekly pay packet'. There are still a few Free Miners at work in the Forest today, coaxing the coal from the seams near the surface and extracting it through what amount to little more than holes in the ground.

Foley's father was a Forest miner – although not of the 'Free' variety – and it was an occupation that eventually claimed his life when he died in a pit fall. Following in a generations-old family tradition, he had started work in the pit as a hob boy, at the age of eleven. Foley's graphic account vividly portrays the extreme hardship of his life underground in those days:

> A chain round his waist and between his legs was attached to a sled, and so he dragged the coal that his step-father had pick-axed out to the bottom of the shaft. It was rare indeed that they worked in a place high enough to stand in. Occasionally there were areas round the base of the shaft high enough to use pit-ponies – creatures that lived, and were often born, under the ground. When they were too weak or too old for work and were brought to the surface, their underground life had made them blind.

* * *

For many years the Forest of Dean gave spiritual sustenance and homely shelter to F.W. (Will) Harvey, one of Gloucestershire's greatest, though sadly neglected, native poets. Harvey was born just north of Gloucester at Murrell's End, Hartpury, in 1888, but spent his childhood and youth at The Redlands, a handsome Georgian farmhouse lying in the water-meadows around Minsterworth, and set well back from the main road opposite what is now The Apple Tree Inn. Harvey's close friend and contemporary, Ivor Gurney, was a welcome and frequent guest at The Redlands from his young days. The two boys had met at the King's School in Gloucester, where Harvey had started as a day boy in 1897, and where Gurney followed three years later. Their lives were to take them in different directions once they left school, but they met again in 1908, when Gurney was articled to the cathedral organist, Dr Herbert Brewer, and they spent a good deal of time together roaming the countryside, and sharing their mutual enthusiasm for books and music. 'Will and Ivor felt themselves to be possessed by Gloucestershire,' explained Anthony Boden in his exhaustive biography, *F. W. Harvey: Soldier, Poet* (1988). 'For them the life-giving air carried the essential balm of Gloucestershire's earth.' He described how, whenever possible, the two young men, both of them aspiring poets, 'would escape together to the welcoming farm at Minsterworth, to help in the fields, to walk in the Severn meadows, to pick fruit in the orchard'. These were rare and precious days indeed for Gurney, whose life was to run such a tragic course. He described Harvey's home in his poem 'The Farm' as:

> A creeper-covered house, an orchard near;
> A farmyard with tall ricks upstanding clear . . .
> Within the house were books,
> A piano dear to me,
> And around the house, the rooks
> Haunted each tall elm tree . . .

Harvey's considerable outpouring of verse from the trenches, and from the prisoner-of-war camp where he was held in solitary confinement, made him a First World War poet to be reckoned with. He published his first collection, *A Gloucestershire Lad at Home and Abroad*, in 1916, and further volumes appeared at regular intervals over the next ten years or so, with considerable success. His name became known to poetry-lovers all over the world from two of his wartime poems, which have subsequently been much anthologized. 'Solitary Confinement' will be familiar to many readers from its opening lines:

> No mortal comes to visit me today,
> Only the gay and early-rising Sun
> Who strolled in nonchalantly, just to say,
> 'Good morrow and despair not, foolish one!'

More famous and idiosyncratic, perhaps, is 'Ducks' ('From troubles of the world/I turn to ducks . . .'), which was inspired by a drawing made by a prison comrade on the dormitory wall. The poem provided the title for Harvey's third book, published in 1919.

Not all of Harvey's poetry, by any means, grew out of his wartime experiences. Much of it celebrated the Gloucestershire landscape of his birth, to an extent that no other poet, except for Gurney, has ever done, and nowhere more lovingly than in 'My Village', Harvey's verse tribute to his childhood home:

> I love old Minsterworth. I love the men;
> The fishers and the cider-makers and
> All who laugh and labour on that land . . .

and in his 'Rondel of Gloucestershire':

> . . . so gleams
> My country, that great magic cup which spills
> Into my mind a thousand thousand streams
> Of glory mellowing on the mellowing hills . . .

After leaving the King's School, Harvey had trained and qualified as a solicitor, a profession to which he returned when he came home after the war. His career took him away from the county for a while, to Swindon, but he was soon back again, living at Cranham ('O Cranham ways are steep and green/And Cranham woods are high'), and working for John Haines in Gloucester. Later, in 1924, after going to work at Haines's Newnham office, he moved to nearby Broadoak, where his unconventional riverside home was a small railway carriage, which lay so close to the water as to be almost on it. During the late 1980s Boden discovered that the poet's old home was still occupied, and the 'friendly owner' explained how in recent years he 'had often been washed out of bed at high tide'! When I made a visit to the same spot in the spring of 1993, however, I found Harvey's former retreat sadly derelict and in the early stages of piecemeal removal to a small railway museum.

From Broadoak Harvey and his family made steady progress deep into the Forest of Dean, renting houses at Whitecroft and Pillowell, before finally settling at Yorkley in 1927. After working for Haines and opening an office of his own at Lydney, Harvey set up practice from his home, but with not altogether favourable results. By that time he was becoming increasingly neglected as a poet, with his books gradually drifting out of print and no new volumes forthcoming.

The writer and poet Leonard Clark, a Cinderford man himself (by upbringing if not by birth),

> A country boy . . .
> Brought up among trees, Forest of Dean,
> coal mines glimpsed over heads of foxgloves . . .

Will Harvey's former riverside home, Broadoak, 1993

who left Gloucestershire to work in London – avowing that 'Absence is the grit in the shell that produces the pearl' – wrote in his volume of autobiography, *A Fool in the Forest*, about the impression Harvey had made on him around that time:

> He had, certainly, except on special occasions, a fine disregard for clothes, and, when among his own familiars, of razors also. I remember him best of all ambling along the country roads, wearing a rather stained navy-blue suit, a battered trilby hat planted firmly on his head, gold-rimmed spectacles on nose, and cigarette between tobacco-stained fingers.

Harvey, in fact, once wrote of himself as 'A thick-set, dark-haired, dreamy little man. Uncouth to see.'

Writing in *Gloucestershire Countryside* just after the Second World War, another local author, Brian Waters, described how he had first met Harvey in one of the poet's favourite settings, the bar parlour of a Forest of Dean inn:

> Some elderly forest miners were talking in their native dialect, so unintelligible to an outsider that it is hardly to be understood, even by those who have lived in Lydney all their lives. Yet sitting among them was a bespectacled man of education, who shared their conversation with fluency and gusto. He was so obviously a Gloucestershire man that you would have taken him for a son of this shire anywhere in the world.

Harvey died in February 1957 and was buried in Minsterworth churchyard. At that time none of his work, except for a few pieces in anthologies, was available, a situation that did not improve for several decades. 'There was a time,' Phelps commented, in the June 1975 issue of *Gloucestershire & Avon Life*, 'when scarcely a drawing-room

Will Harvey's gravestone, Minsterworth churchyard

in Gloucestershire was not graced with a volume of F.W. Harvey's poems. But now he's been so neglected that to many his name means little or nothing.' In recent years, however, there has been a revival of interest in Harvey's poetry, heralded by the unveiling of a tablet to his memory in Gloucester Cathedral in March 1980. His *Collected Poems* were published a few years later and, in 1988, the centenary of his birth was marked by the appearance of Boden's biography.

* * *

Harvey's employer and friend Haines, that 'forgotten genius', as the Cumbrian bard, Norman Nicholson, decribed him in his poem, 'Do You Remember Adlestrop?',

> . . . . who scarcely
> Wrote a line himself but knew the knack
> Of making others write them . . .

was a friend of many poets. As a relative of Lascelles Abercrombie's wife, Catherine, he soon became an intimate of the Dymock colony, and formed particularly close friendships with Edward Thomas and Robert Frost.

As such it is Haines who leads us out of the Forest of Dean and back to nearby May Hill, the steep slopes of which have no doubt felt the tread of umpteen poets over the years. But if it were given to the earth to distinguish between their various footsteps, then those of Haines might well have been the most familiar of all.

When Thomas stayed with Haines for a few days in June 1915, shortly before enlisting in the Artists' Rifles, the two men walked in the Forest of Dean and climbed May Hill just as they had done in Dymock days. While Haines, ever the botanist, went off to examine the plant life, Thomas sat down to write, and produced the first draft of his fine poem, 'Words':

> Out of us all
> That makes rhymes,
> Will you choose
> Sometimes –
> As the winds use
> A crack in a wall
> Or a drain.
> Their joy or their pain
> To whistle through –
> Choose me,
> You English words?

Afterwards Thomas cycled back to his Hampshire home, at Steep, from where he sent Haines a final draft of the poem before setting off to war.

Later, when in August 1928 Frost climbed May Hill again, on a rare foray to England from his American home, it was Haines who was at his side. No doubt Frost raked over some happy memories, as he looked down on the Leadon Valley, recalling those summer days spent at The Gallows and Little Iddens on the eve of the First World War. His recollections would have been tinged with sadness though, by the absence of Thomas, the man who, Frost had once said, was almost more to him than a brother. But Haines was there to provide a link between the two friends, and to connect the past with the present at the top of the powder-blue crescent of May Hill, that eternal symbol of home floating, as Harvey once memorably described it, 'on a flaming sky'.

CHAPTER TWELVE

Cheltenham (1)

When the Hon. John Byng arrived at Cheltenham during a very wet first week of June in 1781, the mineral waters that were to make the town's fortune had already been discovered. In 1716 the presence of a flock of pigeons feeding on grains of salt, in a meadow now occupied by Cheltenham Ladies College, brought to light a saline spring, the water from which was promptly sold for medicinal purposes by the meadow's owner. Later, in 1738, Captain Skillicorne built a small pump room over the spring, but it was to take a visit by George III – out of humour with Bath – exactly fifty years later, and the presence of the Duke of Wellington in 1816, before Cheltenham's reputation as a spa was finally made.

With success came growth, and the town's population of three thousand or so inhabitants in 1800 increased tenfold over the next half-century. Today the number is more than triple that size, and Cheltenham has crept out into the surrounding countryside to claim the once separate villages of Prestbury, Leckhampton and Charlton Kings as suburbs. Daniel Defoe had been quite certain of the town's potential, when he visited Cheltenham during the early years of the eighteenth century. 'The mineral waters lately discovered . . . which are of the Scarborough kind, are what will make this place more and more remarkable, and frequented,' he had prophesied.

Had Byng arrived in Cheltenham a decade or two later, therefore, no doubt he would have been more impressed than he was by the town's elegance, and its well-designed streets and crescents. He would have lingered, perhaps, to make his mark among the fashionable crowds who flocked there to 'take the waters'. Instead he treated it merely as a base from which to explore the neighbourhood, although his excursions were marred once again by incessant rain.

Byng rode out to view the remains of Sudeley Castle, but 'found the road so deep and stoney,' he noted testily, 'as to sicken me of riding that way again'. A few days later he was on Leckhampton Hill, 'the only tolerable way I have yet found', he remarked ominously, but the 'wonderful prospect' of Tewkesbury and the Malvern Hills to his right, with the Severn and the Forest of Dean spread out on his left, seemed genuinely to impress him. But the effect was short-lived: 'This is a truly fine prospect,' he conceded, 'yet prospects please me but for an instant, for they fatigue my eyes, and flurry my nerves, and I allways [sic] wish to find myself in the tranquil vale beneath.'

Breathing a palpable sigh of relief, Byng eventually left Cheltenham on 27 June 1781, declaring wholeheartedly:

I quit thee with pleasure, and hope never more to revisit thee! I believe I may aver and be agreed with, that Cheltenham is the dullest of public places; the look of the place is sombre, the lodgings dear and pitiful, and no inns or stabling fit for the reception of gentlemen or their horses.

The strength of his ill-feeling towards the town renders it all the more surprising, therefore, that we should find Byng lodging in Cheltenham again, exactly three years later to the day. He passed through on his journey from London to North Wales, but his opinion of the place was not improved by the visit, and neither had it stopped raining! On 27 June he recorded:

I attended at the pump room this morning, but neither drank the water, nor embark'd in society, as it wou'd only be a needless trouble. The scenery reminds me of time past, and most things appear at a later day with a worse aspect; the weather, indeed, is so bad as to put all nature out of spirits.

It is difficult to believe, when reading Fanny Burney's account of her visit to Cheltenham four years later, that she and Byng were actually writing about the same place. She noted in her diary:

The birds that chirped, the meadows that bloomed, the hills that rose before us, the purity of the air we breathed, the clearness of the fine blue canopy that covered us, the stillness from turbulence . . . made a union of our faculties with our senses.

Born in 1752, Burney was the daughter of the distinguished musicologist Dr Charles Burney. She married a French émigré, General D'Arblay, in 1793, and published three highly successful novels: *Evelina* (1778), *Cecilia* (1782) and *Camilla* (1796). She was also a prolific writer of lively letters and journals for most of her long life, and it is through these that her spirit shines most clearly.

In 1786 Burney was appointed as Second Keeper of the Robes to Queen Charlotte at a substantial annual salary of £200. It was in this capacity, as a member of George III's household, that she found herself in Cheltenham for a month, during the summer of 1788, when the Court established itself at Fauconberg Hall, facing the Malvern Hills.

George III's visit to the town was, according to Burney, remarkably informal. The King 'took the waters' every morning at six o'clock, then walked about the streets during the day mingling quite freely with the townsfolk, and making himself generally agreeable wherever he went. When he and his entourage finally departed, 'all Cheltenham was drawn out into the High Street,' Burney commented, 'the gentles on one side and the commons on the other, and a band playing "God Save the King" . . . And there ends the Cheltenham adventure.'

Fauconberg Hall, Cheltenham, on the occasion of George III's visit, 1788

But, as T.S. Eliot said, 'the end is where we start from', and, after George III's visit, the town flourished as never before, despite the odium heaped on it by William Cobbett when he visited this great 'devouring Wen' in late September 1826. With manifest contempt he avowed:

Cheltenham is what they call a 'watering-place'; that is to say, a place, to which East India plunderers, West India floggers, English tax-gorgers, together with gluttons, drunkards and debauchees of all descriptions, female as well as male, resort, at the suggestion of silently laughing quacks, in the hope of getting rid of the bodily consequences of their manifold sins and iniquities. To places like this come all that is knavish and all that is foolish and all that is base; gamesters, pick-pockets and harlots; young wife-hunters in search of rich and ugly old women, and young husband-hunters in search of rich and wrinkled or half-rotten men.

Whether his observations were drawn from any kind of scientific research or were merely the result of unshakeable personal prejudice is left for the reader to decide but, understandably, the populace of Cheltenham and the patrons of its efficacious waters were less than impressed by this unseemly outburst, and took their revenge on Cobbett by carrying a burning effigy of him through the streets of the town.

While no one would dispute that Cobbett had stated his case rather too forcefully, giving much offence along the way, there was nevertheless a certain grain of truth in what he had written. By the 1840s Cheltenham had acquired, in some quarters at least, an unenviable reputation as the haunt of fortune-hunters and of the idle rich; a place thronged with visitors whose 'whole life is spent in devising one day how they shall spend the next day with as much enjoyment and as little expense as possible'.

It was not an accusation, however, that could be levelled against that most eminent and Victorian of poets, Alfred Tennyson, who enjoyed an uneasy and intermittent relationship with Cheltenham for much of the 1830s and '40s. It was undoubtedly a difficult period in his life, a time marked by depression, loneliness and a sense of neglect. His close friend, Arthur Hallam, had died in 1833; he was too poor to marry his fiancée, Emily Selwood, and, although his literary reputation was growing, it was not yet widely established. To make matters worse he lost both his own and a substantial amount of his family's money in an unwise business venture that collapsed in 1842. The turning-point in his fortunes, however, was to come in 1850 when *In Memoriam* appeared, confirming Tennyson's poetic stature beyond any doubt. Although still only forty-one he was appointed Poet Laureate – in succession to Wordsworth – that same year, and his success meant that he was able to marry Emily at last, after a long and broken engagement.

The Tennysons as a family had been seeking 'cures' at Cheltenham for several generations by the time Alfred first arrived to sample the therapeutic qualities of the water for himself, in the 1830s. In April 1822 the poet's father had installed himself in the town for a month in an attempt to ward off the worst effects of his excessive drinking. To his wife at home in Lincolnshire he wrote:

> The physician gives me great hopes that the waters will re-establish my health, and says that a schirrus has not yet formed upon my liver, but that he could not have answered for the consequences if I had not immediately come here.

During the autumn of 1843 Tennyson's mother, who was by now a widow, moved to Cheltenham where she settled, together with her unmarried children, at a spacious Regency house in St James's Square. The family had been particularly mobile of late, living at Loughton in Essex, then Tunbridge Wells and Maidstone in Kent, all in a matter of a few years. A restless soul by nature, battling with his twin demons of melancholia and hypochondria, Tennyson spent a great deal of his time away from Cheltenham. However, he was continually drawn back by a sense of obligation towards his mother, and St James's Square was his home, nominally at least, for four years from 1846 to 1850.

Despite his avowed belief in the restorative powers of Cheltenham's medicinal waters, Tennyson found the town's provinciality irritating. 'Here is a handsome town of 35,000 inhabitants, a polka-parson-worshipping place, of which the Revd. Francis Close is Pope,' he wrote to a friend, although adding more generously that it was situated in 'one of the prettiest counties in Great Britain'. Nevertheless, he decamped to London at the least opportunity, unless he was undergoing one of his many 'cures', either in the town itself or at Prestbury – in those days a 'very primitive village', as he described it, but a place that offered the most modern of water-therapy treatments.

On those occasions when he was at home in St James's Square, Tennyson worked in a small study at the top of the house, in a confusion of books and cigarette smoke, looking down on the twenty acres of Jessop's Gardens. It was at this time that he was working on the verses inspired by Hallam's death, and which would eventually comprise *In Memoriam*.

Following his appointment as Poet Laureate in 1850, and his marriage to Emily Selwood, Tennyson contemplated settling in Cheltenham permanently, sharing the tenancy of the St James's Square house with his mother. 'But,' he used to say, 'we Tennysons are a black-blooded race' (no doubt with their tendency towards melancholia in mind), and wiser counsel prevailed. With his wife expecting their first child, he prudently decided to establish a separate home for himself and Emily just outside London.

* * *

Among the various literary visitors who gravitated to Cheltenham during the nineteenth century there grew up in the town two poets whose reputations have now all but faded, but who were, in their time, considered to be among the most original voices of their respective generations. Sydney Thompson Dobell was not a native of Gloucestershire. He was born at Cranbrook, Kent, in April 1824, but by the mid-1830s his family had settled in Cheltenham and Dobell was closely associated with the county for the rest of his life. He spent a part of his childhood at Detmore, in Charlton Kings, not many years before Mrs Craik arrived and turned it into 'Longfield'.

Dobell, who worked from quite an early age in his father's wine business at Cheltenham, relished the contrast that rural Charlton Kings provided with the town. 'Up at seven fishing,' he noted in a typical diary entry of the period. 'A rainy morning, but the country is beautiful, anyhow.'

After his marriage in 1844 Dobell was put in charge of a branch-business at Gloucester by his father, and he went to live in a house called Lark Hay in the nearby village of Hucclecote. His study looked out to the slopes of Chosen Hill – a favourite haunt of two later poets, Will Harvey and Ivor Gurney – and it was in this room during the summer of 1848 that he composed most of his long dramatic poem, 'The Roman', which appeared in 1850, and was his first great popular and critical success.

Dobell completed 'The Roman' at Coxhorne, a substantial mid-eighteenth century house that stands barely a stone's throw from Detmore. With the exception of a conservatory, which was added in more recent years, the external appearance of the house is little changed today from when Dobell and his wife moved there towards the end of 1848.

Late nineteenth-century view of Coxhorne, Charlton Kings

Coxhorne was probably Dobell's favourite among the various houses he was to live in during the remainder of his comparatively short life. 'We are in a lovely valley,' he wrote to his friend Dr Samuel Brown in November 1850, 'beautiful in winter and summer, within a quarter-of-an-hour of the hill-tops and of a view of fifty miles by seventy.'

Dobell and his wife remained at Coxhorne for five years and, in addition to finishing 'The Roman' there, he composed much of his second lengthy dramatic poem, 'Balder', which was published in 1854. He also wrote an appreciative article for a journal, *The Paladium*, about 'Currer Bell', the pseudonym of Charlotte Brontë, whose identity, following the recent publication of *Jane Eyre,* had been the cause of considerable discussion and speculation in London's literary 'salons'. Dobell's 'friendly review', as Brontë later referred to it, led to a lengthy correspondence between Coxhorne and the parsonage at Haworth.

In a letter dated May 1851 Dobell told Brontë:

Lifting my eyes in the sunshine of yesterday to the flowering orchards above me, to the 'summer snow' that stretches away southwards to the hills, and the very Avalon of apple trees that makes an 'awful rose of dawn' towards the east – an impulse seized me to tempt you with a description of their beauty.

He sent her a copy of 'Balder' when it appeared and received an enthusiastic response from the famous novelist. 'I have read him,' replied Brontë in February 1854. 'Remembering well his elder brother, the potent "Roman", it was natural to give a cordial welcome to a fresh scion of the same house and race.'

Although Dobell's two major poems had made a great impact on the reading public and firmly established his literary reputation, he continued to work full time in the family business. But the years that followed were to be dominated by a quest for health, and the need to live in high places and warm climates, especially during the winter months. From his early thirties onwards Dobell's weak lungs often made breathing an effort, so Coxhorne was finally, and reluctantly, given up in 1853 to be replaced, at first by lodgings in Amberley, on the edge of Minchinhampton Common, followed by a long spell in Edinburgh and North Wales.

As Mrs Dobell was in poor health, too, a pattern developed of wintering abroad – usually in the south of France or Spain – until the couple's health became too uncertain even for foreign travel. In the meantime they also lived briefly in various parts of Gloucestershire, for example at Cleeve Tower, with Cleeve Cloud rising impressively behind it. They moved into a new house on Crickley Hill and spent three summers there during the early 1860s. Eventually, however, they were driven away by the unsuitable climate on this 'violent hillside', as Dobell described it, and a brief period in an 'ugly and ill-built' house on the lower slopes of Chosen Hill preceded the Dobells' last move, in April 1871, to Barton End House at Horsley, a mile south of Nailsworth.

Dobell's literary career virtually ceased with his breakdown in health. He published little of note after 'Sonnets on the War' and 'England in the Time of War', which appeared in 1856 and showed his preoccupation with the troubles in the Crimea. Immensely popular in his own day, Dobell's work now, sadly, has little attraction for late twentieth-century audiences.

* * *

Like Dobell, James Elroy Flecker could not claim to have been born in Gloucestershire. Aged only thirty when he died, his short life was filled with travel. If he is associated with any one place in particular, however, then it is with Cheltenham, where he moved – from Lewisham in South London – at the age of two, when his father became the first headmaster of Dean Close School in 1886.

Dean Close School, Cheltenham, c. 1905

Dean Close was Flecker's home for almost half of his life. The nursery where he grew up with his brother and sisters was transformed into his study when he became a pupil at his father's school and, later, an undergraduate at Trinity College, Oxford. The south-facing view, looking over pleasant country towards Leckhampton Hill, was a permanent feature of his childhood and adolescence, and was lovingly evoked in his poem 'November Eves', which appeared posthumously in 1915:

> November Evenings! Damp and still
> They used to cloak Leckhampton Hill,
> And lie down close on the grey plain,
> And dim the dripping window-pane,
> And send queer winds like Harlequins
> That seized our elms for violins
> And struck a note so sharp and low
> Even a child could feel the woe.

Although his early years were punctuated by illness, Flecker was a naturally gifted child – an excellent scholar with a particular aptitude for languages, including the more unusual Arabic and Turkish. He was a keen sportsman and an enthusiastic musician, too, but he was never happier than when he was exploring the Cotswold countryside around his home, usually with his father as a companion. One of their favourite treats was to picnic on Painswick Beacon, even in the depths of winter when, in addition to taking their own food, they would also carry a supply of coal to make tea in a disused quarry they had found during one of their excursions.

Flecker started to write poetry while he was still at school, and produced great quantities of verse during his undergraduate days at Trinity College. His first collection, *The Bridge of Fire*, appeared in 1907, a year before he decided on a career as an interpreter in the consular service. After studying Oriental Languages at Caius College, Cambridge, he was posted to Constantinople during the summer of 1910. But within a few months he became ill. Traces of consumption were found and he was sent back to England to recuperate in a sanatorium at Cranham.

Flecker made a seemingly good recovery once he was back at home in Gloucestershire, and he was able to spend several months visiting family and friends in and around Cheltenham. With the publication of his *Thirty-Six Poems* in 1910 (re-issued in an enlarged edition the following year), Flecker was beginning to establish a considerable reputation. 'Oak and Olive', one of his most enduring poems, belongs to those months at Cranham when, no doubt, his mind was filled with recollections of exploring that same Cotswold country with his father:

> When I go down the Gloucester lanes
> My friends are deaf and blind:
> Fast as they turn their foolish eyes

The Maenads leap behind,
And when I hear the fire-winged feet
They only hear the wind.

Have I not chased the fluting Pan
Through Cranham's sober trees?
Have I not sat on Painswick Hill
With a nymph upon my knees,
And she as rosy as the dawn,
And naked as the breeze?

Flecker also worked on his play *Don Juan* while he was at Cranham, although it was not published until 1925, three years after his celebrated drama *Hassan* was first produced at His Majesty's Theatre in London, with music by Delius.

To all outward appearances fully recovered, Flecker resumed his career in the consular service in 1911, taking up a post in Beirut, where he was to remain for two years. It was there that he absorbed into his writing those Eastern influences that surfaced not only in *Hassan*, but also in his collection of poems, *The Golden Journey to Samarkand*, published in 1913, and for which he is probably best remembered.

In 1913, however, Flecker's health finally gave way, and he spent the last two years of his life at a sanatorium in Switzerland. When he eventually returned to Gloucestershire, in January 1915, it was to be buried on the outskirts of Cheltenham, 'just underneath the brooding Cotswolds,' as his earliest biographer, Geraldine Hodgson, explained, 'encircled by the everlasting hills, in the country he loved best of all'.

CHAPTER THIRTEEN

Cheltenham (2)

The novelist Mrs Craik was staying with friends at Detmore, in Charlton Kings, when she began work on *John Halifax, Gentleman* in 1852–3. It was from there, in fact, that she drove over to Tewkesbury one morning and, on that very first visit, transformed the town into the Norton Bury of her most famous and successful story. But, as any practised novelist would doubtless agree, no experience is truly wasted, and so

Late nineteenth-century view of Detmore, Charlton Kings

Detmore itself became Craik's model for 'Longfield', the country home to which John Halifax moved with his family in more prosperous days, some years before they were to settle at Beechwood Hall in Enderley. Phineas Fletcher, who lived with them, enthused, as always:

Longfield, happy Longfield! Little nest of love, and joy, and peace – where the children grew up and we grew old . . . It was but a small place when we first came there. It led out of the high-road by a field-gate – the White Gate; from which a narrow path wound down to a stream, thence up a green slope to the house; a mere farmhouse, nothing more.

Neither did Cheltenham itself escape Craik's attention. Thinly disguised as 'Coltham', the town was the scene of John Halifax's early, though temporary, fall from grace with his stern employer, the Quaker tanner Abel Fletcher. John Halifax had taken his friend Phineas to the theatre in Coltham one evening to watch Mrs Siddons in a play. The tanner's son recalled:

Near as we lived to Coltham, I had only been there once in my life . . . Before the curtain rose we had time to glance about us on that scene, to both entirely new – the inside of a theatre. Shabby and small as the place was, it was filled with the 'beau monde' of Coltham, which then, patronized by royalty, rivalled even Bath in its fashion and folly.

The nineteenth-century novelist and journalist Robert Surtees, creator of the sporting Cockney grocer, John Jorrocks, was certainly familiar with Cheltenham himself. His series of comic sketches, which appeared in sporting magazines throughout much of the 1830s and were collected as *Jorrocks's Jaunts and Jollities* towards the end of that decade, were an

Cheltenham, c. 1820

obvious influence on Charles Dickens when 'the Inimitable Boz' came to create *The Posthumous Papers of the Pickwick Club*.

The Gloucestershire spa-resort has often been suggested as a possible model for 'Handley Cross', the fictitious town that provided the title, in 1843, for the most successful of Surtees's eight novels. Although it is more likely that Handley Cross was, in fact, an amalgam of several places with which the author was particularly familiar, including Leamington and Brighton, it does not take a great leap of the imagination to realize that Cheltenham fits the bill in many respects. Surtees wrote:

Handley Cross was a pretty village, standing on a gentle eminence about the middle of the Vale of Sheepwash . . . Far to the north the lofty Gayhurst Hills formed a soft and sublime outline, while the rich vale stretched out, dotted with village spires and . . . closed in on either side with dark streaks of woodland.

Everything was suddenly altered, however, when the apothecary Roger Swizzle discovered a mineral spring, which proved to have considerable medicinal properties. Surtees explained:

> The Handley Cross mania spread throughout the land. The village assumed the appearance of a town. A handsome Crescent reared its porticoed front . . . streets branched out, and markets, and lawns, and terraces stretched to the right and the left, the north, the south, the east, and the west . . . A fortune was expended on a pump room, opening into spacious promenade and ballrooms.

There is in that description of Handley Cross undeniably more than a passing resemblance to Cheltenham's own development during the first half of the nineteenth century.

Twenty years after Surtees's account of the growth of Handley Cross, the Reverend Charles Lutwidge Dodgson encountered the Looking Glass House at Charlton Kings. Dodgson, or Lewis Carroll as he is far better known to generations of readers, visited Cheltenham briefly over the Easter holiday at the beginning of April 1863. A brilliant, though rather uninspiring, mathematics don at Oxford, he had been invited to spend a few days with the children of his close friend Henry Liddell, the Dean of Christ Church, who were staying with their grandmother at Hetton Lawn. Dodgson, however, decided to put up at the Belle Vue Hotel in Cheltenham rather than stay at the house itself, although he walked over to Charlton Kings every day.

Liddell's three daughters – Alice, Lorina (Ina) and Edith – were extremely fond of their father's rather shy young bachelor friend, who took them on boating trips and river picnics near their home in Oxford, and who told them entertaining stories – the same stories that were later published with huge success as *Alice's Adventures in Wonderland* and *Through the Looking-glass and what Alice Found there*.

On 4 April 1863 Dodgson recorded in his diary:

> Reached Cheltenham by 11.30am. I found Alice waiting with Miss Prickett [her governess] at the station, and walked with them to Charlton Kings . . . In the afternoon we went a large party in the carriage up to Birdlip, where Ina, Alice and Miss Prickett got out, and walked back with me over Leckhampton Hill. Except for the high wind, the day could hardly have been better for the view.

It was on Leckhampton Hill, as Dodgson confessed later, that his imagination conjured up the Red Queen who was to appear in *Through the Looking-glass*, a character, he said, prompted by Miss Prickett, who was 'the quintessence of all governesses'.

The remainder of the four-day visit was largely uneventful, probably on account of the indifferent weather although, always interested in magic, Dodgson did take the children to a conjuring show in Cheltenham one evening to see what the *Cheltenham Looker-on* described at the time as the 'wonderful tricks and sleight of hand of Herr Dobler, the famous Viennese magician'.

Dodgson's visit to Charlton Kings proved to be one of the last occasions when he was able to spend any great length of time with the Liddell girls, who were by then beginning to grow up. The river picnics that had led to the stories that became, in their turn, *Alice's Adventures in Wonderland*, had taken place a few years earlier, although the book itself was not published until 1865. When it did finally appear, however, the public's appetite for a sequel was enormous, and *Through the Looking-glass* was published with equal success six years later.

Brief though Dodgson's acquaintance with Charlton Kings had been, a curious link was forged between Hetton Lawn and *Through the Looking-glass*. The house possessed – as indeed it still does – a large and ornate overmantel mirror, which is thought to date from the early 1860s and would still have been

Overmantle mirror at Hetton Lawn, the 'Looking Glass House' of Charlton Kings

regarded as something of a novelty when Dodgson paid his visit to the Liddells. While it was certainly not used as a model for Tenniel's famous illustration of Alice walking through the mirror into Looking Glass House, it may well have impressed itself sufficiently on Dodgson's inventive mind to serve as a likely device for Alice's entry into another world of fantasy and imagination.

Although Dodgson related most of the stories in *Through the Looking-glass* to Alice Liddell and her sisters during those same river picnics that had given birth to his earlier masterpiece, it is apparent that the mirror was much on his mind when preparing the sequel, for in a letter written to his friend F.H. Atkinson, four years after that Easter spent at Charlton Kings, Dodgson specifically referred to Hetton Lawn as 'Looking Glass House'.

* * *

Perhaps one of the most flattering appraisals of Cheltenham to appear over the years came from the pen of Dickens, the most eminent of nineteenth-century novelists to visit the town. 'I have rarely seen a place that so attracted my fancy,' he wrote to his old friend William Charles Macready, when the retired actor-manager and the greatest tragedian of his day left Sherborne in Dorset, where he had lived for ten years since quitting the stage, and moved to Wellington Square, at the beginning of 1860. Macready told his friend Sir Frederick Pollock, who later edited the actor's *Reminiscences*:

> Our house is one, as Captain Bobadil [a character in Ben Jonson's *Every Man in His Humour*] would say, 'somewhat of the smallest', after Sherborne, being, I think, not quite a quarter of its size, and it has cost us some trouble to squeeze ourselves and our appurtenances into it . . .

At sixty-seven Macready was attempting to make a fresh start after losing his wife and four of his children all within the space of a few years. He had remarried, and Cheltenham, a town he had played in his theatrical days – and where, less happily, he had been robbed of some valuables by his dresser while performing there on one occasion – seemed an ideal choice as his new home. Perhaps he was also influenced by family considerations. His brother, Major Macready, lived nearby and was later buried in Leckhampton churchyard. Macready wrote:

> I do not think there is a town in England, or out of it, laid out with so much taste, such a continual intermixture of garden, villa, street and avenue . . . that with the shops and clubs and various institutions, gives the promise of a residence answering the demands of the most fastidious.

Macready's arrival at Cheltenham prompted Dickens to visit his old friend there on several occasions, when the famous author gave public readings from his novels in the town. During the final decade of his life, Dickens travelled the length and breadth of Britain, and toured the United States twice, giving his loyal and adoring public what amounted to highly charged one-man shows, rather than just straightforward readings, playing the part of each different character with gusto, and always proving what a natural and accomplished actor he was. Wherever he appeared he attracted capacity audiences, eager, in those days before radio and television, to hear the more famous scenes from his novels brought to life by the very man who had created them. Dickens absolutely revelled in these performances, although they placed an intolerable burden on his health and undoubtedly hastened his death in 1870, at the age of fifty-eight.

Dickens had made his Cheltenham debut in October 1859, only a few months before Macready moved there, as the novelist explained in a letter to Macready the following January:

I had never seen [Cheltenham] before. Also, I believe the character of its people to have greatly changed for the better. All sorts of long-visaged prophets had told me that they were dull, stolid, slow, and I don't know what more that is disagreeable. I found them exactly the reverse in all respects.

Dickens returned to Cheltenham on at least five occasions during the 1860s, deliberately including the town in each of his reading tours for Macready's benefit. He invariably performed at the now demolished Assembly Rooms where, as in every town and city where he appeared, the murder scene from *Oliver Twist*, involving Bill Sikes and Nancy, met with the best audience reaction.

Not even Macready, who had been an unrivalled Macbeth in his day, was immune to Dickens's hypnotic stagecraft, no matter whether he was enacting the death of little Paul

Dombey or the trial scene from *The Pickwick Papers*. After
one performance the old actor exploded:

> I swear to Heaven that, as a piece of passion and playfulness,
> indescribably mixed up together, it does amaze me as
> profoundly as it moves me. But as a piece of Art – and I have
> seen the best Art in a great time – it is incomprehensible to
> me. How it is got at, how it is done, how one man can – well!
> It lays me on my back, and it is of no use talking about it.

Dickens's farewell performance at Cheltenham was given in
January 1869, when both he and Macready were already in
failing health. Presenting the scene between Sikes and Nancy
for the very last time, 'Boz' was at his most inimitable, and
Macready thoroughly appreciated the performance, declaring
that it was equal to 'two Macbeths'! The two old friends never
met again, as Dickens died eighteen months later. Although
extremely frail, Macready lingered on until the spring of 1873
when, as the *Cheltenham Looker-on* reported in its issue dated
3 May, the old actor, aged eighty,

> Of no disease, of no distemper died,
> But fell like Autumn fruit that mellowed long;
> Even wondered at because it fell no sooner.

CHAPTER FOURTEEN

Gloucester

'Gloucester,' declared the poet Samuel Taylor Coleridge somewhat unkindly, in the days of his youthful republican ardour, 'is a nothing-to-be-said-about town.' But his dismissive attitude can no doubt be partly excused on the grounds that the future author of 'Kubla Khan' and 'The Rime of the Ancient Mariner' was merely passing through, and fired at the time with the white heat of Pantisocracy, the scheme he devised with Robert Southey to set up a commune in New England. In 1794 twenty-two-year-old Coleridge had places to go and things to see, and Gloucester, one senses, was not high on his list of immediate priorities.

Clearly, Coleridge did not linger, as other literary travellers have done over the years, to savour the delights of the Cathedral: Norman in origin but much remodelled and beautified in medieval times, with its magnificent pinnacled tower added during the fifteenth century. Even today it is the very core of the city, and an instantly recognizable landmark for miles around.

Those doughty travellers, Celia Fiennes and Daniel Defoe, both remarked on the cathedral's famous 'whispering place'. 'Speake never so low just in the wall at one end, the person at the other end shall heare it plaine, tho' those which stand by you shall not heare you speake,' explained Fiennes conspiratorially. 'It's the wall carrys the voyce,' she added. Defoe, however, was not quite so impressed with the novelty of it all. 'Experience has taught us the easily comprehended reason for the thing,' he remarked, loftily, 'and since there is now the like in the church of St Paul, the wonder is much abated.'

Almost as famous as the city's cathedral, however, The Bell Inn was the somewhat incongruous birthplace, in 1714, of George Whitefield, the great eighteenth-century Methodist preacher and disciple of Charles Wesley. The Bell was subsequently kept by Whitefield's brother and, when Henry Fielding's Tom Jones arrived there one evening, after being thwarted in his intention to reach Bristol, he was greeted by a host who was, declared Fielding,

> absolutely untainted with the pernicious principles of Methodism, or any other heretical sect. He is a very honest plain man and, in my opinion, not likely to create any disturbance either in Church or State. His wife . . . might have made a shining figure in the politest assemblies.

The Bell Inn, Gloucester, c. 1830

There was nothing very polite, however, about the welcome she accorded the unfortunate Geoffry Wildgoose and Jerry Tugwell some years later, when they found themselves seeking shelter at The Bell after their trials and tribulations on Dover's Hill:

'Hey day', quoth Mrs Whitefield, 'lodgings indeed! Yes, to be sure; because Squire Fielding, forsooth, in that romancing book of his, pretends that Tom Jones was harboured here, we shall be pestered with all the trampers that pass the road.'

Surprisingly, though, when John Byng stayed a night at The Bell it went entirely, and uncharacteristically, without comment, although he could not resist the urge to take a swipe at the cathedral. 'The tower,' he conceded, 'is very handsome and very light; which is more than can be said of the pillars in the body of the church, which seem gouty and immoderately swelled.'

* * *

Over the past four hundred years or so Gloucester has produced three native poets; men of vastly different temperaments whose lives took diverse courses, and for only one of whom, Ivor Gurney, was the city and its surrounding countryside truly an abiding theme. Since his death at a Kent mental hospital in 1937, Gurney's posthumous reputation has grown, to secure his place not only as Gloucester's own Poet Laureate, but as its tragic genius, too.

John Taylor, the so-called 'Water-poet', was the earliest of this motley trio. Born in the ancient parish of St Ewins during August 1580, very few details have survived concerning his family background or his Gloucester childhood, so that we are left today with only the faintest impression of the man. *The Dictionary of National Biography* informs us – not surprisingly, given his subsequent career – that Taylor came of 'humble origins', and that he was sent as a pupil to both the grammar school in Gloucester and the Crypt Grammar School, the latter of which had been founded in 1539.

However, before long Taylor was apprenticed to a Thames waterman in London – how or why we can have no idea – working on a river that, as the main artery through the capital, was thronged with people and cargo of all descriptions. Taylor's own estimate, that there were forty thousand such watermen working on the Thames between Windsor and Gravesend, gives some indication of the scale of activity on the river in those far-off days.

Unfortunately Taylor's apprenticeship was cruelly interrupted when he was press-ganged into the navy. He served under the Earl of Essex and was present, when still only a young lad of sixteen, at the siege of Cadiz in 1596. After retiring from the service with a leg injury a few years later, he took up his duties as a fully-fledged waterman on the Thames, although he was eventually forced to find alternative work as fierce competition made it difficult to earn a decent living. Later, it seems, he worked as a publican, initially in Oxford and then in London's Covent Garden.

From an early age Taylor had capitalized on his natural ability to write doggerel verse as a means of supplementing his income and, as the years went by, his work attracted the admiration of some distinguished contemporaries, including Ben Jonson. Much of Taylor's output, however, was only of ephemeral interest and quickly forgotten after publication. His most enduring piece, perhaps, was an account in verse of his trip down the Thames, made in a rowing-boat, from the river's source in Gloucestershire all the way to London:

No place in England could a treasure keepe,
Thames to maintain, but Coteswould (queene of sheepe).

Taylor died in 1653, over seventy years of age and landlord of the self-styled Poet's Head in Long Acre. Here an inscription composed by the 'Water-poet' himself, and emblazoned on the sign hanging above the entrance to his inn, epitomized Taylor's workmanlike attitude to the art of 'sweet poesy':

> There's many a head stands for a sign,
> Thou gentle Reader, why not mine?
> Though I deserve not, I desire
> The laurel wreath, the poet's hire.

W.E. Henley, like Taylor, is a somewhat shadowy figure these days – a familiar name that is hard to place. Yet in his time he was not only a well-known poet, but also a distinguished editor, critic and anthologist. He was born in the very heart of Gloucester at 2 Eastgate in 1849, and lived for nearly half of his fifty-four years within sight of that famous old crossroads of which Eastgate forms one arm.

Eastgate Street, Gloucester, 1889

Henley certainly had a literary start in life, in the sense that, like Dr Johnson before him, he was the son of a bookseller, a not altogether successful businessman whose pressing debts continually drove his family from one temporary address to another: from Eastgate to Southgate, on to St John's Lane, then back to Eastgate, in an endless procession.

After spending his early schooldays at Suffolk House, in the centre of Gloucester, and later moving out to Newark House in nearby rural Hempsted, Henley became a pupil at the Crypt Grammar School when he was eleven. For three years his headmaster was the famous Manx poet T.E. Brown, who was the author of that immortal, if somewhat inscrutable, line, 'A garden is a lovesome thing, God wot.' It was to prove a most significant meeting for teacher and pupil alike, and one that was to have repercussions throughout their lives. 'This episode,' Henley explained some years later, 'opened to me the ways of thought and speech, and discovered me the beginning, the true materials, of myself. What [Brown] did for me was to suggest possibilities in life and character as I had never dreamed.' As Brown must surely take some credit for revealing the poet in Henley, so in later years the younger, distinguished man of letters was able to repay his old headmaster by commissioning essays from him for various journals, and writing a preface for Brown's *Collected Poems* when they appeared in 1900.

Shortly after enrolling at the Crypt Grammar School, Henley was attacked by tuberculosis, a disease that was to pursue him relentlessly over the years. He lost one foot while still only in his teens, and it was the search for a cure that finally, and permanently, took him away from Gloucester during his early twenties, when he became a patient at Edinburgh Infirmary in 1873, to be placed under the care of Joseph Lister.

By this time, of course, Henley was already contributing essays and verse to a number of periodicals, including the *Cornhill Magazine*, whose editor in those days was Virginia

Woolf's father, Leslie Stephen. When Henley had been at the infirmary for over eighteen months, Stephen called on him there, while visiting the city. He wrote to his wife in 1875:

> I had an interesting visit to my poor contributor. He is a miserable cripple . . . who writes poems of the Swinburne kind. I went to see [Robert Louis] Stevenson this morning, and told him all about this poor creature, and am going to take him there this afternoon.

When Stevenson duly arrived in the ward, Henley 'sat up in his bed, with his head and beard all tangled', recorded the author of *Treasure Island,* 'and talked as cheerfully as if he had been in a king's palace'.

Henley and Stevenson became close friends at once. They were not only almost exact contemporaries, but also writers, and fighting the same disease too. Their friendship led to collaboration on a number of plays, none of which was particularly famous although *Deacon Brodie*, written in 1880, did achieve some measure of popularity when it was produced in the United States a few years later. Of more obvious interest, perhaps, is the fact that Stevenson confessed to having based his character of Long John Silver on Henley's 'boisterous and piratic' nature.

When Henley was eventually discharged from Edinburgh Infirmary he moved to London, where his prolific output of articles and poetry found a ready home in *The Athenaeum* and *The Pall Mall Gazette*. In 1888 he became the editor of the *National Observer*, moving to the *New Review* six years later. He compiled the seven-volume *Dictionary of Slang* and produced several collections of his own poetry, from which little has survived over the years, with the honourable exception of the still much anthologized 'Invictus', a response to his days in Edinburgh Infirmary, the opening stanzas of which are still capable of making most spines tingle:

Out of the night that covers me,
Black as the pit from pole to pole,
I thank whatever gods may be
For my unconquerable soul.

In the fell clutch of circumstance
I have not winced nor cried aloud.
Under the bludgeonings of chance
My head is bloody but unbowed.

Henley died in June 1903 following a railway accident, and thus he unwittingly defeated his old enemy, tuberculosis. Although he had been born in Gloucester he was, like Taylor, not essentially a Gloucestershire poet. But at the time of Henley's death there was growing up in the ancient minster city a young lad who was destined to become both a poet and a composer, and for whom the county of Gloucestershire was to be his constant source of inspiration.

Ivor Gurney was born on 28 August 1890 at 3 Queen Street, in a house that was demolished long before the Second World War. His father was a tailor and, shortly after his son's birth, he moved to 19 Barton Street, slightly larger premises that were both shop and home to David and Florence Gurney, and their four children.

Gurney attended the National School in London Road, but it was when he started Sunday School at All Saints' in 1896 that he first came to know Alfred Cheesman. This was the man who, as a young curate, had served as the infant Gurney's godfather and who was to play probably the most important role in the boy's early life. Cheesman immediately encouraged him to join the All Saints' choir as a probationer, and Gurney's voice was judged to be so fine that, by the autumn of 1900 – prompted by Cheesman to compete for a place – he had become a member of the Cathedral Choir.

As a choirboy at Gloucester Cathedral Gurney became a pupil at the King's School. He was an adequate but unexceptional scholar with a healthy interest in games. At first there was little to distinguish him from the other boys, but, under Cheesman's continuing influence and guidance, Gurney developed interests that drew him away from both his friends and his family.

As he grew into adolescence it became obvious to everyone who knew him that Gurney possessed exceptional musical ability. It was also at about this time that Gloucestershire began to exert a strong hold over him. As a young boy he had relished the regular Sunday evening outings with his family to

> Maisemore's delightful ridge, when Severn flowing
> Nourished a wealth of lovely wild things blowing
> Sweet as the air – . . .

and where his grandmother lived in that Severn-side village a mile or so north of the city.

During his teens, however, Gurney started wandering farther afield, and usually alone. Sometimes he would walk all day then sleep out at night, finding shelter where he could, under a hedge or in a barn. On other occasions he would turn up at the house of a friend – more often than not Will Harvey's home at Minsterworth – usually in the early hours of the morning, and 'camp out' on the living-room floor. 'It was useless to interfere,' recalled his sister, Winifred. 'The truth was, he did not seem to belong to us . . . He simply called on us briefly, and left again without a word.'

In 1906, after he had left the Gloucester Cathedral Choir, Gurney was articled to the cathedral organist, Dr Herbert Brewer. The composer Herbert Howells was a fellow pupil, and the two boys got on well together. Gurney soon learned to play the organ. He was seventeen, and a career as a professional musician seemed inevitable. He had begun composing in 1904 and, although this early work was of little merit, it gave a fair indication of the way in which he was developing musically. Therefore it was no great surprise when, in 1911, he won a scholarship to The Royal College of Music in London.

In a sense the college was to prove a mixed blessing for Gurney. On the positive side he could not have wished for a more splendid opportunity, studying composition under Sir Charles Stanford; but on the negative side student life took him away from his beloved Gloucestershire. 'Digs' in Fulham were no substitute for the winding Cotswold lanes, and occasionally the need to return home overwhelmed him. In May 1913, on the verge of a nervous breakdown – a precursor to the more serious and sustained mental illness he was to suffer later – Gurney escaped to the Lock House at Framilode, close by the Severn, for self-healing. 'And as for Framilode,' he wrote to Marion Scott, the musicologist who had befriended him at college, 'who could do justice to it? . . . Oh what a place! Blue river and golden sand, and blue-black hills – in fine weather of course! London is worse than ever to bear after that!'

River Severn at Framilode, 'Homing again to the sea'

Away from London and Gloucestershire, however, international events were conspiring to change the course of Gurney's life, and the lives of millions of other young men of his generation. In 1914, at the outbreak of the First World War, Gurney volunteered for the army but was turned down owing to poor eyesight. In 1915, when he offered himself again, he was accepted, and joined the 2nd/5th Gloucesters. He left for France in May of the following year and, on Good Friday 1917, he was wounded. Later that summer he went to Ypres, and was gassed at Passchendaele that September.

It was hardly a unique story – millions suffered as Gurney did, and many fared worse. What marked him out, however, was the fact that, throughout his time at the Front, living and fighting in the horror of the trenches, he was writing poetry – poems that were, just like his friend Harvey's, at once both a response to the war and a celebration of, and a yearning for, his native Gloucestershire.

Gurney's first book of war poems, *Severn and Somme*, was published to good reviews in November 1917. Craving indulgence from his readers for any roughness of technique that they may discern, he explained in the preface that the images of beauty in his mind, when writing these poems 'in France, and in the sound of the guns . . . were always of Gloucester, county of Cotswold and Severn, and a plain rich, blossomy and sweet of airs':

> God, that I might see
> Framilode once again!
> Redmarley all renewed,
> Clear shining after rain.
>
> May Hill that Gloster dwellers
> 'Gainst every sunset see;
> And the wide Severn river
> Homing again to the sea.

Gurney had returned to England by the time his second volume, *War's Embers*, appeared in 1919, and, although life in the trenches had taken its toll, he was able to resume his course at The Royal College of Music, where he continued his studies under Ralph Vaughan Williams. By the following year, however, Gurney's erratic behaviour was the cause of some disquiet among his close friends. Although it was a very creative time for him – he was composing a great deal of music including songs, piano pieces and an orchestral work – he had grown increasingly restless, and his solitary wanderings became extensive. Sometimes, on the spur of the moment, he would walk from London to Gloucester, or spend the night sleeping out on the Embankment. Although still a student at The Royal College of Music, he spent most of the spring and summer of 1921 living in an old Cotswold stone cottage on Dryhill Farm, Witcombe, in the shadow of Crickley Hill. Gurney had written in the trenches:

> If only this fear would leave me I could dream of Crickley
>   Hill,
> And a hundred thousand thoughts of home would visit my
>   heart in sleep.

When Gurney left college in 1922, having failed his final examinations, he went back to Gloucester. He stayed either with friends or simply slept out-of-doors, before moving in with his brother, Ronald. For much of the time he was unemployed but, when he did occasionally obtain work – for example as a cinema pianist and in the Gloucester office of the Inland Revenue – he found it impossible to hold down the job.

Gurney's behaviour became increasingly unpredictable and, after making an attempt at suicide, he was eventually admitted to Barnwood House, a private convalescent home for the mentally ill, in Gloucester. Before long, however, his condition had deteriorated further, and he was transferred to the City of

London Mental Hospital at Dartford, Kent, where he was to remain for the rest of his life. Gurney wrote a great deal of poetry during the long months and years that he was incarcerated in a locked ward. Many of these 'asylum poems', as they have become known, found their way into Marion Scott's hands, and she succeeded in placing a number of them with various periodicals during Gurney's lifetime.

It was Scott, in fact, who arranged for Helen Thomas, Edward Thomas's widow, to visit Gurney in hospital when she took along some old Ordnance Survey maps of Gloucestershire, maps that had once belonged to her husband. Thomas recalled later:

> This proved to have been a sort of inspiration, for Ivor Gurney at once spread them out on his bed and he and I spent the whole time I was there tracing with our forefingers the lanes and byways and villages of which Ivor Gurney knew every step and over which Edward had walked.

Gurney was a great admirer of Thomas's poems, and he set some of them to music. Surprisingly the two men had never met, despite their mutual acquaintance with Lascelles and Catherine Abercrombie during the old Dymock days.

After being virtually ignored for years – something that is the 'common lot of genius' according to the Northamptonshire poet John Clare, who ended his days in an asylum similarly neglected – Gurney died just at the time when his work was beginning to receive wider attention. Tuberculosis killed him while the first two volumes of his songs were being prepared for publication by Oxford University Press. More volumes followed, and new selections of his poetry have appeared over the years, culminating in the publication of his *Collected Poems* in 1982.

After his death Gurney's body was taken back to Gloucestershire, his beloved native county, which he had not seen for fifteen years.

> Do not forget me quite,
> O Severn meadows,

he had once written, and so he was buried in Twigworth churchyard, close to the river and in that land of flat water-meadows just north of Gloucester. Cheeseman was there at the last – just as he had been at the beginning – to conduct the funeral service on New Year's Eve 1937.

* * *

It would be interesting to learn if, as a young boy wandering through the city streets of Gloucester near his home, during the late 1890s, Gurney had ever glimpsed a well-built, rosy-cheeked and rather matronly young lady, sitting on a pavement with easel and sketch-pad set out in front of her, and gazing intently at the scene around her. If so, the young artist in question might easily have been Beatrix Potter, at work on some preliminary drawings for her story *The Tailor of Gloucester*.

Ivor Gurney's gravestone, Twigworth churchyard

Potter's famous tale was actually, though loosely, based on a true incident, concerning a real-life Gloucester tailor called Mr Prichard. He had been commissioned to make a waistcoat for the new mayor of the city – a waistcoat that His Worship was to wear at his first official function: leading a procession from the Guildhall to the Shire Hall, on the occasion of the annual Root, Fruit and Grain Society Show. As Prichard's wife explained some years later, her husband was inundated with work at that particular time and, on the Saturday prior to the show, he had gone home leaving the waistcoat, still unfinished, lying on his workbench. When Prichard arrived at his shop on the following Monday morning he found, to his delight, that the garment had been completed in his absence, except, that is, for one buttonhole. In fact, the tailor's assistants had gone back to the workshop while their employer was away, to finish off the waistcoat as a surprise. They pinned a note against the unfinished buttonhole, which read 'No more twist!'.

Unable to think of any other likely explanation for his good fortune, Mr Prichard light-heartedly attributed it to the fairies, and placed an eye-catching notice to that effect in his shop window. When Potter heard this affecting tale, however, the fairies instantly became mice and *The Tailor of Gloucester* was born.

As was to prove the case with each of her many books, Potter took meticulous care over the drawings she made to illustrate her story, ensuring that they were accurate in every detail. So, whenever she visited Harescombe Grange to stay with the Huttons, she found the opportunity to drive into Gloucester and make background sketches of various streets and buildings, with a view to using some of the material she gathered in her final illustrations.

College Court, one of the most instantly recognizable scenes in *The Tailor of Gloucester*, with its archway leading through to College Green, is now home to the small Beatrix Potter Museum, housed in the premises that Potter herself used as a

College Court, Gloucester, now the home of the Beatrix Potter Museum

model for the tailor's home, although this was not where Prichard actually lived. Furthermore the interior of the tailor's workshop was not sketched in Gloucester at all, but in Chelsea some time later. To compound the illusion *The Tailor of Gloucester* is set at Christmas, with College Court and the whole city wrapped in snow. Yet most of Potter's sketches were made on hot summer days, though it would be impossible to guess from the finished drawings.

The Tailor of Gloucester was, according to Potter, her own favourite among the many books she wrote for children. It first appeared in 1902 in a privately printed edition of five hundred copies and was published by Frederick Warne the following year. As for Mr Prichard, he died in 1934 – though not before he had become a footnote in literary history – and was buried at Charlton Kings, where his tombstone was inscribed to 'The Tailor of Gloucester'.

CHAPTER FIFTEEN

Bristol (1)

> There were three sailors of Bristol City
> Who took a boat and went to sea.
> But first with beef and captain's biscuits
> And pickled pork they loaded she.

These opening lines from William Thackeray's famous poem about 'Little Billee' serve to provide more than just a hint of the illustrious sea-going past of Bristol, a port on the River Avon,

> . . . a street of masts,
> And pennants from all nations of the earth,
> Streaming below the houses, piled aloft
> Hill above hill . . .

wrote the parson poet William Bowles in 1829. Once known as the 'birthplace of America', owing to the thousands of early settlers in the New World who sailed from this cathedral and, nowadays, university city, Bristol has enjoyed close links over the centuries with the neighbouring county of Gloucestershire. The relationship was physically severed by the administrative change in boundaries that led to the creation of Avon in 1974, but, inextricably woven together as they are – historically, commercially and socially – some account of Bristol's literary connections provides a logical, perhaps even essential, accompaniment to a literary tour of Gloucestershire.

This is not to imply, however, that Bristol lacks an important and significant literary tradition of its own – far from it. The city, after all, was the birthplace of Thomas Chatterton and Robert Southey, as well as being the cradle of Pantisocracy. Neither should it be forgotten that an enterprising Bristol bookseller, Joseph Cottle, was the person responsible, in 1798, for publishing *Lyrical Ballads*, a joint collection of poetry by William Wordsworth and Samuel Taylor Coleridge, which was to prove a landmark in the annals of the English Romantic Movement.

Those events were very much in the future, however, when the seventeenth-century diarist, John Evelyn, arrived in Bristol with his wife during the summer of 1654. A prominent churchman and an ardent Royalist, Evelyn was an author of some diversity, producing work on – among other topics – arboriculture, navigation and smoke pollution in London. He is chiefly remembered today, however, for his memoirs, which were first published in 1818, more than a hundred years after his death.

Evelyn's visit to Bristol was no more than a brief excursion from Bath, where he was spending a short holiday. The city and port were soon destined to become the largest in England after London, much of Bristol's prosperity at that time being derived somewhat ignominiously from the slave trade, which had grown up around the home demand for sugar and tobacco. This state of affairs was reflected in Evelyn's diary entry for the occasion. 'Here,' he recorded, 'I first saw the manner of refining sugar, and casting it into loaves, where we had collation of eggs fried in the sugar furnace, together with excellent Spanish wine.'

Just over a decade later that most famous and readable of all diarists, Samuel Pepys, arriving in Bristol with his wife and servant, Deb Willet, declared the city 'in every respect another London'. It was the summer of 1668, and, like Evelyn before him, Pepys and his entourage were staying at Bath. The prospect of a day trip to explore the nearby thriving city that he had long wished to see proved irresistible, and was made

Broad Quay, Bristol, c. 1735

even more so by the fact that Willet's uncle, William Butts, was a wealthy Bristol merchant, Willet herself having been born in in the city's lowly Marsh Street.

For Pepys his visit was more than enhanced by the generous hospitality displayed by Willet's uncle, in whose company the famous diarist, with his professional interest in all things naval, explored the Custom House and the quays, and was able to inspect a new vessel then under construction. 'It will be a fine ship,' he confidently pronounced.

Later, Pepys and his wife were conducted to a surprise meal, which had been laid on for them at Butts's house: 'a good entertainment,' drooled Pepys, afterwards, 'of strawberries, a whole venison pasty cold and plenty of brave wine and above all "Bristoll Milk" '. The qualities of this delectable local beverage, so Pepys was informed, were preserved by the drawing of carts on sledges rather than wheels, thereby minimizing the disturbance caused to the 'golden velvet wine', as it was described, which lay in the cellars below the cobbled streets. 'We back and by moonshine to the Bath again about 10 o'clock,' recorded Pepys in undeniably mellow mood later that evening.

Both Celia Fiennes and Daniel Defoe visited Bristol in the wake of the irrepressible Pepys, and Defoe was full of admiration. It was, he recorded,

the greatest, the richest and the best port of trade in Great Britain, London only excepted. The merchants of this city not only have the greatest trade, but they trade with a more entire independency upon London, than any other town in Britain. And 'tis evident in this particular, (viz.) that whatsoever exportations they make to any part of the world, they are able to bring the full returns back to their own port, and can dispose of it there.

As though this eulogy were not sufficient in itself, the city harbours a distinctly more tangible connection with the famous author of *Robinson Crusoe*. Candlesticks on the altar of Bristol Cathedral are said to have been presented as thanksgiving gifts by privateers who picked up Alexander Selkirk – the Scotsman on whom Defoe based his immortal character – after his lonely sojourn on the Juan Fernandez Islands.

During her visit to Hotwells in 1698, Fiennes investigated the curative spring below St Vincent's Rocks, on whose celebrity the growth of Georgian Clifton was founded. In its heyday, during the late eighteenth century, Hotwells proved to be one of the most popular spas in Britain, much patronized by royalty and the aristocracy. 'The water,' recorded Fiennes, 'lookes exceeding cleer and is as warm as new milk and much of that sweetness.'

St Vincent's Rocks, Hotwells, Bristol, c. 1792, from a water-colour by J.M.W. Turner

Half a century earlier, having digested his collation of eggs fried in the sugar furnace, Evelyn had ventured into the same area, an experience that seems to have left him dumbfounded. He declared:

> But what was most stupendous to me was the rock of St. Vincent, the precipice whereoff is equal to anything of that nature I have seen in the most confragose cateracts of the Alpes; the river gliding betweene them at an extraordinary depth.

As the popularity of Hotwells increased, so a number of literary visitors arrived over the years to experience for themselves the curative properties of its medicinal waters, enhanced by the bracing air of Clifton Down. Inevitably this trend was reflected in some of the fiction of the period.

In 1767, as a girl of fifteen, Fanny Burney visited Hotwells with her father. They stayed for only three days, but long enough for her to be sufficiently impressed by the place and to employ it as a setting for some of the later scenes in her first novel, *Evelina*, which was published anonymously in 1778. Written in the epistolary form popular at that time, *Evelina*, which was an immense success as soon as it appeared, recounts the fortunes of the eponymous heroine who, left to all intents and purposes an orphan, is raised by her guardian. After falling in love with the handsome Lord Orville, the unravelling of a complicated plot eventually allows her to marry him. In the midst of all this uncertainty, however, Evelina falls ill, and is despatched to Bristol Hotwells in order to effect her recovery. 'We are situated upon a most delightful spot,' Evelina informs her friend, Maria Mirvan. 'The prospect is beautiful, the air pure, and the weather very favourable to invalids. I am already better, and I doubt not that I shall soon be well.'

It is undoubtedly a reflection of the Hotwells's enormous popularity at the time that Matthew Bramble and his entourage eventually arrived there in 1771, during the course of Tobias Smollett's last, and possibly finest, novel, *Humphry Clinker*. Again written as a series of letters, the irascible and hypochondriac Bramble was scouring the country in search of health. Possessing a less sunny disposition than Evelina, however, he found that the famous health-giving resort fell somewhat short of his expectations. Soon after arriving he told his friend Dr Lewis:

> I have read all that has been written on the Hot Wells, and what I can collect from the whole is, that the water contains nothing but a little salt, and calcarious earth, mixed in such

inconsiderable proportion, as can have very little, if any, effect on the animal economy. This being the case, I think the man deserves to be fitted with a cap and bells, who for such a paultry advantage as this spring affords, sacrifices his precious time, which might be employed in taking more effectual remedies, and exposes himself to the dirt, the stench, the chilling blasts, and perpetual rains, that render this place to me intolerable.

Not even an invigorating hack across Clifton Down could redeem the situation as far as Bramble was concerned. Thus, he berated Lewis, in whose professional opinion a breath of fresh air had clearly seemed desirable,

I rode out upon the Downs last Tuesday . . . when the sky, as far as the visible horizon, was without a cloud; but before I had gone a full mile, I was overtaken instantaneously by a storm of rain that wet me to the skin in three minutes . . . It makes me sick to hear people talk of the fine air upon Clifton Downs. How can the air be either agreeable or salutary, where the demon of vapours descends in a perpetual drizzle?

On the other hand the playwright Richard Brinsley Sheridan, author of that most durable of English comedies *The School for Scandal*, seemed to possesss an almost unshakeable faith in the restorative powers of the Hotwells. Yet during the course of his tragic visits in 1787 and 1792, both his wife and his sister-in-law died from consumption, a condition that was reputed to be particularly responsive to the water that issued out of St Vincent's Rocks.

Sheridan's often poignant letters from the period recount their own sad story of the raised and dashed hopes of his wife's last, tortuous weeks. He informed the Duchess of Devonshire in a letter dated 7 May 1792:

> We got here safely yesterday, and she has borne the latter
> part of the journey amazingly well, and appears much
> better today. Dr. Bain, a young physician lately settled here
> and who came here himself in a consumption is reckon'd
> very skilful in these cases.

For some weeks Mrs Sheridan's life hung in the balance, as
she rallied and deteriorated by turns. Sheridan kept their
friends well informed about her progress – or, rather, the lack
of it! 'Very poorly today,' he told Lady Duncannon on 16 May.
'I cannot describe to you how sunk I am.' Then, four days
later, he was able to report more cheerfully that his wife was
'pretty well', after weathering another crisis and receiving
further treatment. The ordeal finally ended in late June,
however, when Mrs Sheridan succumbed to the inevitable and
died.

The novelist Maria Edgeworth became enmeshed in a
convoluted series of literary connections around Hotwells and
Clifton during the 1790s. Brief though her family's association
was with the area, sufficient time elapsed for her sister Anna to
marry a local physician, Dr Beddoes, who was both doctor and
friend to Southey, Wordsworth and Coleridge, and whose own
son, Thomas Lovell Beddoes, born in 1803, subsequently
became a poet and dramatist, and the author of *Death's Jest-
Book*. This macabre collection of poems, with its emphasis on
the supernatural and human decay, was begun in 1825 but did
not appear until a quarter of a century later, shortly after its
author had committed suicide. One of the younger medical
attendants assisting with out-patients at the Pneumatic
Institute, a health establishment founded by Dr Beddoes in
Dowry Square, was Peter Mark Roget, whose name is still
synonymous with his world-famous *Thesaurus*, which was first
published in 1852.

When Edgeworth arrived in Clifton during the summer of
1791 she was in search of a cure for her younger brother's

consumption. She lodged with her family at Prince's Buildings, and spent a great deal of time either hunting for fossils on the nearby downs or coaxing her ailing younger brother to 'take the waters'. A prolific writer for over forty years, Edgeworth was born in 1768 and lived for most of her life at the family home in County Longford, Eire. Probably best remembered nowadays for her historical novel *Castle Rackrent*, 'the great Maria', as Sir Walter Scott called her, also published several volumes of children's stories. Clearly she possessed the born writer's natural instinct for storing up experience and turning it to good use, because a couple of those tales were found to have a Bristol background. One was set at Long Ashton, a short distance from the city, and another recounted the adventures of two boys who lodged with their uncle at Prince's Buildings and took part in an archery contest on the downs.

* * *

One of Bristol's most celebrated literary visitors during the nineteenth century was undoubtedly Charles Dickens, who first arrived in the city as a young reporter on the *Morning Chronicle*, during November 1835, when he covered the Stroud by-election in which Lord John Russell was the government candidate. Russell was to make an important speech in Bristol, and Dickens, who had firmly established himself as the fastest shorthand writer in the Parliamentary Press Gallery, was despatched from London to report the details for his newspaper.

Dickens, who in addition to his journalistic work was also in the throes of preparing his first book, *Sketches by Boz* (a collection of previously published essays, culled from the various periodicals in which they had appeared), lodged at The Bush Inn, a hostelry that stood close to the Guildhall until the former was demolished during the mid-nineteenth century. And so it was, perhaps, no mere coincidence that when, in Dickens's second book, *The Pickwick Papers*, published in 1837, Mr Winkle found it advisable to quit Bath hurriedly in fear of his

The Bush Inn, Corn Street, Bristol, c. 1825, from a drawing by T.L.S. Rowbotham

life from a jealous husband, and to seek refuge amid the clamour of Bristol, he too should take up his headquarters at The Bush.

Soon after his arrival, however, Winkle learned that Arabella Allen, a young lady to whom he was desperately romantically inclined, happened to be staying somewhere in the vicinity of Clifton and the Downs. Eager to gain a personal interview with her at all costs, he enlisted the help of Sam Weller, Mr Pickwick's indefatigable servant, to track her down, Weller having by this time arrived from Bath in pursuit of Winkle!

The following morning, as Dickens records:

Sam Weller issued forth upon his quest, in no way daunted by the very discouraging prospect before him; and away he walked . . . we were going to say, up one hill and down another, only it's all uphill at Clifton – without meeting anything or anybody that tended to throw the faintest light on the matter in hand.

Sam struggled across the Downs against a good high wind, wondering whether it was always necessary to hold your hat on with both hands in that part of the country . . .

Eventually, however, his rugged determination was rewarded, when he reached a group of secluded houses where he found not only Arabella, but Mary, the pretty housemaid from Ipswich, with whom Sam had enjoyed an earlier flirtation of his own.

On a later occasion in the crowded and complicated history of the Pickwickians, Pickwick and Weller found themselves again at The Bush, and Mr Winkle's love life was once more the issue at stake. It was on this visit that Pickwick was regaled with the 'Story of the Bagman's Uncle', by the one-eyed Bagman himself, over a glass of negus one evening in the travellers' room of that old Bristol inn. The following morning Pickwick and his friends set off to Birmingham, on the journey that took them *en route* to The Hop Pole at Tewkesbury.

Many years after the advent of *The Pickwick Papers*, Dickens was to visit Bristol on various occasions in his capacity as an amateur actor and as a professional reader of his own works. In November 1851 he arrived with a touring theatrical company, which comprised mainly enthusiastic relations and friends – including another famous novelist, Wilkie Collins, author of *The Moonstone* and *The Woman in White* – to give a couple of performances of Edward Bulwer-Lytton's play *Not So Bad as We Seem*. The proceeds were intended to swell the coffers of the Guild of Literature and Art, an ultimately unsuccessful scheme devised by Dickens and Bulwer-Lytton to assist impoverished writers and their families. 'We never played to a better audience,' enthused Dickens, after his group of strolling players had given their opening performance at the Victoria Rooms, Clifton. 'The effect of from thirteen hundred to fourteen hundred people, all well dressed and all seated in an unbroken chamber . . . was most splendid.' He wrote to tell his wife that the members of the company, 'well lodged and boarded and, living high up on the Downs, are quite out of the filth of Bristol'!

But it was in the course of his public reading tours that Bristol came to know Dickens best of all. These exhausting performances took him to the city several times during the last twelve years of his life, and his presence never caused less than a sensation. During an electrifying evening at the Victoria Rooms in August 1858, 'the people,' wrote Dickens, 'were perfectly taken off their legs by "The Chimes" – started – looked at each other – started again – looked at me – and then burst into a storm of applause'.

Predictably the murder scene involving Bill Sikes and Nancy from *Oliver Twist* worked its old familiar magic, too, as Dickens reported to his daughter after a performance in January 1869, during his farewell tour:

At Clifton on Monday night we had a contagion of fainting, and yet the place was not hot. I should think we had from a dozen to twenty ladies taken out stiff and rigid, at various times! It became quite ridiculous.

In January 1850 Dickens's old friend, the tragedian William Macready (who, at Cheltenham had declared the murder scene equal to 'two Macbeths'!), gave his last performance in Bristol, shortly before he retired from the stage completely. He had played the city many times over the years, and the occasion was marked by an emotional farewell speech to the audience after the performance of *Henry IV* had ended. 'On silence,' he recorded in his diary, later the same evening, 'I addressed them, quite overcome by recollections, the present cordiality and my own feelings to "good old Bristol" . . . So farewell to my dear old Bristol audiences – most warmly and affectionately do I remember them.'

Perhaps T.E. Brown, who had been W.E. Henley's mentor at the Crypt Grammar School in Gloucester, was present at one of Dickens's Bristol readings. One suspects, however, that the daemonic fury with which 'the Inimitable Boz' assailed his audience on these occasions might have been too much for the self-effacing Manx poet, who was a housemaster at Clifton College for almost thirty years from 1864. It was a lengthy career, about which he clearly entertained some reservations:

> I'm here at Clifton grinding at the mill,
> My feet for thrice nine barren years have trod . . .

Brown eventually retired to his native Isle of Man, but Clifton claimed him in the end when he died on a visit there in 1897. Curiously he enjoys an oblique connection with one of the more famous episodes in Bristol's literary history. In *Treasure Island* Robert Louis Stevenson sends his young narrator, Jim Hawkins, to eighteenth-century Bristol, where the lad finds himself wandering among the labyrinth of teeming quays. He declared:

Though I had lived by the shore all my life, I seemed never to have been near the sea till then. The smell of tar and salt was something new. I saw the most wonderful figureheads, that had all been far over the ocean. I saw, besides, many old sailors, with rings in their ears, and whiskers curled in ringlets, and tarry pigtails . . .

The Llandoger Trow, King Street, Bristol

172

Later, Jim is despatched to The Spy-Glass, 'a little tavern with a large brass telescope for a sign', in search of its landlord, the one-legged Long John Silver. 'He was very tall and strong,' Hawkins explained, 'with a face as big as a ham – plain and pale, but intelligent and smiling.'

The Hole in the Wall, a popular eighteenth-century waterside pub, is thought to be the prototype of The Spy-Glass. Similarly The Admiral Benbow, kept by Jim Hawkins's father, is alleged to have been modelled on The Llandoger Trow, a gabled tavern in King Street, converted from three seventeenth-century houses where Defoe, on a visit to Bristol, is reported to have met Alexander Selkirk. More to the point, however, Stevenson himself acknowledged that his friend Henley was the inspiration behind Long John Silver, thereby establishing Brown as the former headmaster of probably the most famous buccaneer in literary history!

CHAPTER SIXTEEN

Bristol (2)

My own loved Clifton, jocund May
Hath decked thy banks and bowers again,
Thy populous elms that crowd the plain,
Thy birches, fountains of green spray.

Clifton will probably never have a more ardent literary champion than the nineteenth-century poet, essayist and critic John Addington Symonds. Born in 1840, the son of an eminent physician, he suffered from tuberculosis and lived for much of his adult life in Switzerland and Italy. His childhood, however, was spent in one of Clifton's most opulent mansions, Clifton Hill House, a mid-eighteenth century building, which is now in the hands of Bristol University.

Symonds was born at 7 Berkeley Square and lived there until he was eleven, but it was the lighter and more spacious Clifton Hill House that claimed his heart, and the home he looked back on so lovingly throughout his life. Forty years after first setting foot in the house he could still vividly recall the June day in 1851 when his father had taken the family to their new home:

I entered the solemn front door, traversed the echoing hall, vaulted and floored with solid stone, and emerged upon the garden at the farther end . . . For us it was like passing from the prose of fact into the poetry of fairyland.

Nervous and withdrawn, and frequently ill during his childhood, Symonds's introspection helped to develop his imagination wonderfully, and the prospect from Clifton Hill House over the city of Bristol spread out below – in the mid-nineteenth century a vista rich in masts and church spires – for several years represented the extent of his world. From his bedroom window he watched the dawn break, and revelled in the vagaries of the weather in all its moods the seasons round. Once he was privileged to see a comet, 'a thin rod of amber white, drowned in the saffron of sunset'. Writing to his daughter from Davos, towards the end of his life, he told her:

> I sometimes yearn for what I always had at Clifton, the sun rising above a mighty city, flooding wood & pasture & sea-going river, & all the many works of men – the sun setting in glory beyond that strip of sea & low Welsh hills, with the wonderful tenderness of pure yellow spaces & tremulous stars.

After being educated at Harrow and Balliol College, Oxford, Symonds was forced to abandon his legal studies in London because of poor health and the need to seek a friendlier climate abroad. Later he returned to live in Clifton, at 7 Victoria Square, and, after his father's death in 1871, he went back to Clifton Hill House, which still remained in the family. By then married himself, Symonds returned to his childhood home, doubting the wisdom of the move. 'The feelings with which we are settling down here are very mixed,' he wrote to his sister. 'It is almost painful to find again, the same yet not the same.'

Symonds and his wife, Catherine, remained at Clifton Hill House until 1880 and, during those nine years, following in the family tradition of dispensing excellent hospitality, they entertained numerous visitors in their elegant home. A fellow poet, Sydney Dobell, who in those days shortly before his death was living at Horsley in south Gloucestershire, was always a welcome guest. Dobell had spent several winters at Clifton over the years for the benefit of his health and, being under Dr Symonds's care on those occasions, had known the physician's son as a young boy.

Eventually Symonds's health broke down irretrievably, enforcing a permanent move to Switzerland. The family home, together with all it contained, was sold. 'For a long time I felt very sore – like a soldier crab without his shell,' Symonds confided to a friend. 'I fancy I shall not care for any home again.'

A prolific essayist and poet in his day, Symonds's largest work was *Renaissance in Italy*, which appeared in six volumes (1875–86). He also published studies of, among others, Percy Shelley, Walt Whitman and Sir Philip Sidney, not to mention many travel sketches, including portraits of Italy, Greece and Switzerland. Much closer to home, however, he saw through the press, just before he died in 1893, a collection of essays, *In the Key of Blue*, which included a piece called 'Clifton and a Lad's Love', where the title speaks for itself. Here was a Clifton viewed through the eyes of an aesthete and a classical scholar, but none-the-less recognizable for all that: as he clambers down St Vincent's Rocks, the cliff shining 'like marble in her plenilunar splendour', or wanders through sheets of bluebells in the clearings of Leigh Woods. 'Clifton, now as ever, is full of vague yet powerful associations,' he wrote, wistfully. 'When will this Circe cease to brew enchantments for my soul?'

* * *

If it could ever truthfully be said that Bristol once enjoyed a golden literary age, then it must surely have been during the second half of the eighteenth century, the turbulent years of Thomas Chatterton, Robert Southey and Samuel Taylor Coleridge. But there were also several supporting players on the stage, to lend both depth and colour to the scene.

Hannah More, an extremely popular and dauntingly prolific writer on mainly religious and moral themes, was born in the schoolhouse at Fishponds in 1745. Regarded as something of an infant prodigy by her parents on account of her remarkable

School House, Fishponds, Bristol

capacity for learning, she later joined her three elder sisters in the management of a school that they had opened in Trinity Street, and at which More had been a pupil herself. The school, founded in 1757, proved a great success, a flourishing intellectual centre, in fact, which drew the attention of many distinguished visitors to Bristol. As a habitual writer of stories from an early age, it was not long before the young schoolmistress became a published author. With the appearance of her first play, a pastoral drama called *The Search for Happiness*, the die was cast and More's writing career was successfully launched.

In 1774 More embarked on the first in a series of annual visits to London, where she quickly established herself as an eminent member of the Blue Stocking Circle. To her delight she found that one introduction swiftly led to another and, as a result, she made an impressive list of friends, including the actor David Garrick, the novelist Samuel Richardson, and the renowned Dr Johnson.

At the height of her literary fame, and shortly before she turned almost exclusively to the writing of improving and religious tracts from the seclusion of her home at Cowslip Green, More was introduced to the poetry of a young Bristol dairywoman – or 'milkwoman', in the local terminology of the day – called Ann Yearsley. Born in Clifton in 1752, Yearsley, married with five children and very poor, had been inspired by her mother since childhood with a passion for books and reading, something that was altogether unusual in those comparatively unenlightened days for one of her calling and circumstances. When More, on returning to Bristol in the autumn of 1784, was shown some of the milkwoman's poetry, she was highly impressed. 'The verses,' she told a friend, 'breathed the genuine spirit of poetry and were rendered the more interesting by a certain natural and strong expression of misery which seemed to fill the heart and mind of the author.'

More enthusiastically raised subscriptions among her many influential friends, and Yearsley's first collection, *Poems on Several Occasions*, was duly published in 1785, to some extremely kind reviews – not least from Horace Walpole and the Bristol bookseller and publisher Joseph Cottle. Some plays and novels appeared over the years, together with further volumes of poetry, including *The Rural Lyre* in 1796, but by that time Yearsley was swiftly heading back to the obscurity from which she had been plucked a decade earlier.

Soon after the publication of *Poems on Several Occasions*, Yearsley had taken exception to the fact that the subscriptions that had been raised on her behalf were put into a trust, thus denying her the opportunity to spend her capital as she wished. The situation arose from a simple misunderstanding, but accusations and counter-accusations flew between the trustees and the wounded milkwoman. 'I felt as a mother deemed unworthy of the tuition and care of her family,' she wrote, a touch melodramatically. At one stage she even accused the blameless More of attempting to misappropriate the funds in order to buy a country house.

Although far from entirely discredited by this controversy, it took the shine from Yearsley's subsequent literary career. She was able to set herself up in a circulating library for a while, in Hot Wells Crescent, and publishers were still found for her work. However, a series of personal tragedies and the exhaustion of her thin vein of talent meant that Yearsley's death in 1806 passed virtually unnoticed, except for the waspish epitaph quoted by J.M.S. Tompkins in his essay 'The Bristol Milkwoman' (1938):

> Ann Yearsley tasted the Castalian stream
> And skimmed its surface as she skimmed her cream;
> But struck at last by fate's unerring blow
> All that remains of Ann is – 'Milk Below'.

In contrast, More died full of years and honour. The poems, essays, tracts and novels of her Somerset years – spent at Cowslip Green and, later, Barley Wood – were not only unashamedly uplifting, but also widely popular, with some of her titles selling millions of copies. In 1828, towards the end of her prodigiously long life, More moved back to Bristol to a home at Windsor Terrace in Clifton where, five years later, she died at the age of eighty-eight.

* * *

More was barely seven when, in 1752, a baby was born in Pile Street (now Redcliffe Way), the son of a recently deceased schoolmaster and his impoverished seamstress widow. 'Holy Hannah', as she was dubbed by one rather unkind wit, was still only twenty-five when that same boy, as an adolescent of seventeen, was found dead – killed by his own hand – in an attic room at 39 Brooke Street, Holborn. A famous painting of the tragic scene, executed by Henry Wallis almost a century after the event, succeeded in camouflaging the unpleasant

Thomas Chatterton's birthplace, Redcliffe Way (formerly Pile Street), Bristol

nature of the business by investing Chatterton – for it was he – with a romantic air, his body lean with near starvation stretched out on its deathbed. It was an image that did much to establish Chatterton as the cult figure and folk hero that he more or less remains today.

Pitifully – and needlessly – brief though his life was, Chatterton still managed to earn himself a national reputation; the first Bristol poet, in fact, to do so. It is an exquisite irony, therefore, that he committed suicide simply because he felt himself to be neglected, but, like many a genius before him and afterwards, his reputation was acquired entirely posthumously.

Chatterton's interest in heraldry and antiquities – an abiding passion that was to prove the source of his fame and of his undoing – was probably inherited from his schoolmaster father. It was further nourished by the easy access he enjoyed to the nearby church of St Mary Redcliffe where, after generations of Chattertons had been sextons there, the young boy was not only baptized but also, as he grew older, spent hours combing through the parchments and old parochial documents that filled the chests in the muniment room over the church porch. These excursions into an essentially medieval world provided him with a diverting contrast to the somewhat lame and, by all accounts, uninspiring teaching he received at the Blue-Coat charity school attached to Colston's Hospital, from where it was the norm for pupils to become apprentices.

However, Chatterton's great interest in reading and his obsession with the past marked him out from an early age as an unusually bright scholar. He was only ten when his first poem was published in a local Bristol newspaper, a rare feat by any standards, but even more remarkable given his unpromising background.

Nothing, however, could halt his inexorable progress towards an apprenticeship and, when he left Colston's at the age of fourteen, he started work in the Corn Street office of a Bristol lawyer called John Lambert. It was an excellent beginning for a boy in Chatterton's position, but he did not view it in that light and he found the copying of legal documents irksome. Hating the work and indignant at being regarded as no more than an ordinary servant, almost on a level with the pot boy, or so he thought, he found some outlet for his anger among a group of like-minded young souls, forerunners, had they but known it, of the locksmith Gabriel Vardon's anarchic apprentice, Simon Tappertit, in Charles Dickens's *Barnaby Rudge*.

But it seemed as though Chatterton's years of research, poring over the crumbling and dusty old manuscripts in the muniment room of St Mary Redcliffe, were at last going to pay off, with the boy still only in his mid-teens. He had been composing so-called 'antique' poems for some years and had succeeded in duping several people, including the usher at his school, into believing that they were the genuine, hitherto undiscovered works of various medieval poets. By chance he encountered a group of gullible local worthies – Burgum, a pewterer, Catcott, his assistant, and Barrett, a surgeon, appear to have been, for a variety of reasons, the most vulnerable –

and plied them with historical documents and poems purporting to come from the chests in the muniment room. Chatterton also wrote and published fictitious transcripts of local historical events, provided Burgum with a false genealogy and, most notorious of all, released from time to time a series of poems that he supplemented with pseudo-scholarly footnotes and explanations of obscure points, declaring them to be the work of one Thomas Rowley, an entirely imaginary fifteenth-century Bristol poet and priest. He was said to have been a close friend of William Canynge, a wealthy Bristol merchant, who contributed generously to the rebuilding of St Mary Redcliffe.

It was the authenticity of these so-called 'Rowley' poems that was to exercise the mind of many a literary scholar for years after Chatterton's untimely death. In 1776, for example, no less a luminary than Dr Johnson, in the company of his friend and biographer, James Boswell, made an excursion to Bristol to investigate the Rowley manuscripts personally, 'on the spot'. It was not the first occasion that the good doctor had enquired into a literary forgery. Three years earlier, during his 'grand tour' of Scotland and the Western Isles, he had flatly contradicted the authenticity of various epic poems reputed to be the work of an ancient Gaelic bard called Ossian, believing them more likely to be the product – in large measure, at least – of the fertile imagination of their 'translator', James MacPherson. Now it was Chatterton's turn to undergo scrutiny.

Perhaps Johnson remembered during his brief sojourn in Bristol that thirty years earlier his good friend, the wayward and impecunious poet Richard Savage, had died a pauper's death – an echo of Chatterton's own fate – in the city's Newgate Prison. Savage, a complicated personality with delusions of grandeur, was on his way from London to Wales to spend his life in rural seclusion away from all the temptations that the metropolis had to offer. He was provided with a small annuity by his friends, who hoped that his writing would flourish in the country, but Savage got no farther than Bristol, where he swiftly plunged into debt and, shortly afterwards, died mysteriously in prison. The *Life of Mr. Richard Savage*, which first appeared in 1744, was one of Johnson's early major works and it was reissued over thirty years later in his celebrated collection, *The Lives of the English Poets*.

On their arrival in Bristol, Johnson and Boswell were met at their inn by George Catcott, whereupon Johnson, according to Boswell, then

> read aloud some of Chatterton's fabricated verses, while Catcott stood at the back of his chair, moving himself like a pendulum, and beating time with his feet, and now and then looking into Dr. Johnson's face, wondering that he was not yet convinced.

Later the three men called on Barrett the surgeon and, together, this unlikely quartet repaired to the muniment room

Muniment Room, St Mary Redcliffe, Bristol, c. 1843, from a drawing by S.G. Tovey

at St Mary Redcliffe so that Johnson and Boswell might see for themselves the chest from which these literary treasures had been gleaned. Johnson, however, was not persuaded and remained highly sceptical of the manuscripts' medieval origin. 'This is the most extraordinary young man that has encountered my knowledge,' he said of Chatterton. 'It is wonderful how the whelp has written such things.'

Although Chatterton had enjoyed a rare success in passing off his own compositions as the work of Rowley and his contemporaries – and even though he was engaging in a fraud, Chatterton's historical knowledge and poetic genius should not be underestimated in one so young – he received scant payment for all of his efforts. In 1770, unable to find a patron for his work, he decided to try his fortunes in London where he enjoyed some small success for a short time, contributing political articles with an anti-government flavour to a variety of sympathetically minded journals. After a few months, however, this avenue of employment came to an end and Chatterton grew poorer as each day passed. Too independent to accept offers of food or other practical assistance, and despairing of achieving literary fame, he committed suicide on 24 August 1770. He had been in London for only four months.

* * *

Within a few years of Chatterton's death two budding poets were born – one of them in Bristol – for whom 'the marvellous Boy/The sleepless Soul that perished in his pride', as William Wordsworth described him was, in one way or another, to have a certain significance. In October 1772 Coleridge 'sprang to light' in a Devon vicarage at Ottery St Mary. For over forty years he worked intermittently at his 'Monody on the Death of Chatterton', a poem he first published while still an undergraduate at Cambridge. It was a piece of work he continually revised and added to throughout his career. In August 1774 Southey was born over his father's draper's shop at 9 Wine Street, in the very heart of Chatterton's native city.

As a young boy the spectre of Chatterton hovered over Southey and drew him irresistibly to St Mary Redcliffe. 'Poor Chatterton,' he lamented, 'oft do I think upon him and sometimes indulge the thought that had he been living he might have been my friend.' In 1803 Southey edited Chatterton's *Collected Works* so that the proceeds could go to the boy poet's impoverished family. Coleridge and Southey were destined to become close friends as young men, and the story of an important episode from the early days of their volatile relationship serves to provide the city of Bristol with what is arguably its most important literary encounter of all.

After a peripatetic childhood, spent partly with a formidable aunt in Bath and partly at home in Bristol, a rich uncle paid for Southey to attend Westminster School, where his refusal to conform eventually resulted in his expulsion. Despite this, however, he was admitted to Balliol College, Oxford, where he soon acquired a reputation as a radical and revolutionary young man and where, during the summer of 1794, he was visited by Coleridge, a like-minded undergraduate from Cambridge, who, in common with Southey, was struggling to become a poet.

The two men, who had been introduced by a mutual friend, got on together famously, to such an extent, in fact, that the impulsive Coleridge, who was about to set off on a long walking tour of Wales, delayed his departure for three weeks, and spent the intervening time with Southey, concocting a plan to set up a democratic commune on the banks of the Susquehanna River in New England. The scheme, which quickly took on a momentum of its own, was called Pantisocracy, a venture, it was envisaged, that would comprise twelve young gentlemen and twelve young ladies, all living together in close harmony on the land, and with each member of the group having an equal share in the government of the enterprise.

It was an intensely idealistic vision, born of two impulsive young men – though Southey was shortly to prove himself quite otherwise – in the heat of full-throated summer. For the moment, however,

Coleridge set off on his arduous hike through the Welsh mountains and Southey returned, for once in high spirits, to Bristol, to recruit likely Pantisocrats. In the excitement and novelty of it all, Coleridge could not resist adding a stanza to his 'Monody':

> Oh Chatterton! that thou were yet alive!
> Sure thou woud'st spread the canvass to the gale
> And love with us the tinkling team to drive
> O'er peaceful Freedom's undivided dale . . .

Southey, lodging with his Aunt Tyler in College Green, immediately set about generating interest in Pantisocracy among his Bristol friends and, before long, Coleridge joined him in the city to add his practical support. For Coleridge it proved to be a visit of the utmost significance, both in personal and professional terms, for it was on this occasion that he met Joseph Cottle, the bookseller and publisher whose shop stood on the corner of Corn Street and High Street. To this young man fell the distinction of publishing the first works by Wordsworth, Coleridge and Southey, although to Cottle it must have seemed a dubious privilege at times, as he hinted after the publication of Wordsworth's and Coleridge's *Lyrical Ballads* in 1798. 'The sale was so slow and the severity of the reviews so great,' he explained, 'that its progress to oblivion seemed ordained. I parted with the greatest proportion of the [edition] at a loss, to Mr. Arch, a London bookseller.'

During those heady summer days of 1794, Southey also introduced his new friend to the Fricker sisters, a family of five girls who lived with their widowed mother in genteel poverty. Later, Edith Fricker was to marry Southey, and Sara would become Coleridge's wife, but for the moment they were all ardent Pantisocrats and yearning for the day when they would emigrate to a new life on the banks of the Susquehanna.

Cottle did all he could to advance the cause of Pantisocracy, and to swell the coffers of the emigrants' funds, by offering to

Corner of Corn Street and High Street, Bristol, early nineteenth century (the building with the curved façade was formerly Joseph Cottle's bookshop), from a drawing by George Delamotte

publish any poems that Southey and Coleridge might write, and by arranging for them to give courses of lectures in Bristol. But as summer merged into autumn and winter drew on, the fortunes of Pantisocracy declined with the seasons. The beginning of 1795 found Southey and Coleridge sharing cramped lodgings in College Street, where the two friends wrote their poetry and prepared lectures at the same table, and argued endlessly over the finer points of their scheme. 'Our names,' Southey told another friend at the time – somewhat prematurely, as it turned out – 'are written in the book of destiny on the same page.'

The temperamental incompatibility that surfaced during their shared life in College Street, however, sounded the death-knell for any plan that might require the close co-operation of Southey and Coleridge. Over the months Southey discovered that his friend's chaotic and indolent lifestyle sat uneasily with his own naturally more organized approach. Coleridge was to remain a maverick all his life, but Southey, like Wordsworth, was destined to settle into long years of conventional gentility.

By the following September the dream of Pantisocracy had evaporated; Coleridge and Southey had quarrelled bitterly and gone their separate ways. They were soon to be united again, however, when Coleridge married Sara Fricker at St Mary Redcliffe in October 1795, and Southey married her sister, Edith, in the same church just over a month later.

In the weeks immediately prior to his wedding, Coleridge was given the opportunity to meet another poet, a man whom he had long admired from a distance and who was passing through Bristol *en route* for Dorset. Twenty-five-year-old Wordsworth was on his way to Racedown Lodge to set up home for the very first time with his doting sister, Dorothy; an arrangement that was to endure for over half a century – mostly at Grasmere in the Lake District – until Wordsworth's death in 1850.

Wordsworth stayed for five weeks at 7 Great George Street, the town house of a rich sugar-merchant called John Pinney,

No. 7 Great George Street, Bristol, from a drawing by A.C. Fare

who owned Racedown Lodge and whose sons were close friends of the future Poet Laureate. It was there, at what is now the Georgian House Museum, that Coleridge and Wordsworth first met briefly. Wordsworth wrote to a London friend afterwards:

> Coleridge was at Bristol part of the time I was there. I saw little of him. I wished indeed to have seen more – his talent appears to me very great. I met with Southey also. I recollect your mentioning you had thought him a coxcomb. This surprises me much, as I never saw a young man who seemed to have less of that character.

Following their first meeting an intense friendship developed between Wordsworth and Coleridge. Professionally it was a mutually productive relationship, symbolized in their collaboration on *Lyrical Ballads*.

In the meantime, after his wedding and a long honeymoon spent in a sequestered cottage at Clevedon, Coleridge had returned to Bristol where, for a brief period, he planned and edited a radical newspaper called *The Watchman*, setting up his headquarters at The Rummer tavern in High Street. As with many of Coleridge's projects, however, the novelty soon palled under the weight of the day-to-day work, and the final issue appeared in May 1796. A few months later he settled at Nether Stowey in Somerset, with Sara and their young son, Hartley.

After his marriage to Edith, Southey left immediately for Portugal, but he was soon back in Bristol, staying with his wife in lodgings at an address 'care of Joseph Cottle'. Plans to study the law were abandoned and, in June 1798, the Southeys moved to a house at Westbury-on-Trym,

> a filthy, old barn-looking house, in the pleasantest part of this country. The view over the garden is very beautiful, a fertile and woody vale bounded on each side by hills two

miles distant . . . Ten minutes' walk would convey me to one of the most beautiful glens I ever saw.

They called the house Martin Hall (owing to the number of house-martins that nested in the eaves) and lived there for a year. It proved to be a most fruitful period for Southey. He wrote prolifically during those twelve months and produced some of his most famous ballads, including 'The Well of St. Keyne' and 'St. Michael's Chair'. Cottle published a volume of his poems, together with new editions of some earlier works: *Joan of Arc* and *Letters Written During a Short Residence in Spain and Portugal*. He was also undertaking regular reviewing work for several periodicals.

The Southeys left Martin Hall when their lease expired, but it was not without regret. A few years afterwards as the tenant of Greta Hall in Keswick – where he lived from 1802 until his death in 1843 – Southey wrote to a friend that 'Bristol is still the place to which I must cling – very often do I remember Westbury and wish the years that are past could return.' Once, in 1836, he did revisit Westbury-on-Trym, only to find that Martin Hall had been demolished some years earlier.

* * *

Two hundred years have elapsed since Southey and Coleridge were to be found frequenting the lodging-houses and meeting halls, and the crowded taverns of Bristol's close streets – two centuries that have wrought change to the city on such a grand scale as to render it barely familiar to those long-dead poets were they able to see it now. When J.B. Priestley alighted at Temple Meads Station during the course of his *English Journey*, it is just possible that the city he encountered in the 1930s had more in common with the Bristol of the late-eighteenth century than has the sprawling metropolis of today with that same city of sixty years ago. The wholesale destruction of the Second World War and the massive rebuilding programme that followed it have seen to that.

Happily, though, the spirit of Bristol remains sufficiently intact for Priestley's brief assessment to be as relevant now as ever it was. 'Bristol,' he wrote, 'is a fine city. It is a genuine city, an ancient metropolis. As you walk about in it you can wonder and admire. The place,' he declared, 'has an air.'

Select Bibliography

In addition to those sources already mentioned, the following works proved invaluable during the preparation of this book:

Archer, Fred, *The Village of My Childhood*, Alan Sutton, 1989.

Beckinsale, R.P., *Companion into Gloucestershire*, Methuen, 1939.

Boden, Anthony, *F.W. Harvey: Soldier, Poet*, Alan Sutton, 1988.

Burney, Fanny, *Evelina,* Tauchnitz, 1850.

Byng, John, *The Torrington Diaries* (Ed. C. Bruyn Andrews), Eyre & Spottiswoode, 1934/8.

Carroll, Lewis, *The Diaries* (Ed. R.L. Green), Cassell, 1953.

Clark, Keith, *The Muse Colony*, Redcliffe Press, 1992.

Cobbett, William, *Rural Rides*, Penguin, 1967.

Cottle, Basil, *Robert Southey and Bristol*, Historical Association, University of Bristol, 1980.

Craik, Mrs, *John Halifax, Gentleman* (1856), J.M. Dent, 1961.

Defoe, Daniel, *A Tour Through the Whole Island of Great Britain* (1724/6), Webb & Bower/Michael Joseph, 1989.

Dexter, Walter, *The England of Dickens*, Cecil Palmer, 1925.

Fiennes, Celia, *The Journeys* (Ed. C. Morris), MacDonald/Webb & Bower, 1982.

Gibbs, J. Arthur, *A Cotswold Village* (first published 1898), Alan Sutton, 1988.

Graves, Richard, *The Spiritual Quixote*, publisher unknown, 1772.

Graves, Richard Perceval, *The Scholar-poet*, Routledge & Kegan Paul, 1979.

Grosskurth, Phyllis, *John Addington Symonds*, Longman, 1964.

Hodgson, Geraldine, *The Life of James Elroy Flecker*, Oxford University Press, 1925.

Holmes, Richard, *Coleridge: Early Visions*, Hodder & Stoughton, 1989.

Jolly, E., *The Life and Letters of Sydney Dobell* (2 Vols), Smith, Elder, 1878.

Jones, M.G., *Hannah More: a Biography*, Cambridge University Press, 1952.

Macready, W.C., *Reminiscences*, (Ed. Sir Frederick Pollock), Macmillan, 1876.

Meyerstein, E.H.W., *A Life of Thomas Chatterton*, Ingpen and Grant, 1930.

Smith, Constance Babington, *John Masefield: a Life*, Oxford University Press, 1978.

Smollett, Tobias, *The Expedition of Humphry Clinker* (1771), Collins, 1954.

Thomas, Helen, *A Memory of W.H. Davies*, Tragara Press, 1973.

Thomas, Helen, *As it Was and World without End*, Faber & Faber, 1972.

Thurston, E. Temple, *The Flower of Gloster* (1911), Alan Sutton, 1984.

Tompkins, J.M.S., *The Polite Marriage*, Cambridge University Press, 1938.

Whitfield, Christopher, *Robert Dover and the Cotswold Games*, Henry Sotheran, 1962.

Williamson, Kennedy, *W.E. Henley: a Memoir*, Harold Shaylor, 1930.

Index of People and Places